D1236314

Puzzles and Paradoxes in Economics

'... men are fond of paradoxes, and of appearing to understand what surpasses the comprehension of ordinary people ...'

Adam Smith

To our two favourite paradoxes, Jo Ann and Jackie

Puzzles and Paradoxes in Economics

Mark Skousen

Adjunct Professor of Economics and Finance, Rollins College

and

Kenna C. Taylor

Associate Professor of Economics, Rollins College

Edward Elgar Publishing
Cheltenham, UK · Brookfield, US

© Mark Skousen and Kenna C. Taylor 1997

All rights reserved. No part of this publication may be reproduced, stored in a retrieval system, or transmitted in any form or by any means, electronic, mechanical, photocopying, recording, or otherwise without the prior permission of the publisher.

Published by
Edward Elgar Publishing Limited
8 Lansdown Place
Cheltenham
Glos GL50 2HU
UK

Edward Elgar Publishing Company
Old Post Road
Brookfield
Vermont 05036
US

A catalogue record for this book is available from the British Library

Library of Congress Cataloguing in Publication Data
Skousen, Mark.
    Puzzles and paradoxes in economics / Mark Skousen and Kenna C.
Taylor.
    Includes bibliographical references and index.
    1. Economics. 2. Microeconomics. 3. Macroeconomics. 4. Finance.
5. Marketing. 6. Paradox. 7. Puzzles.   I. Taylor, Kenna C., 1945–.
    II. Title.
HB 199.S54   1997
330–dc20   96–42202
                                                                          CIP

ISBN 1 85898 378 9

Printed and bound in Great Britain by
Biddles Limited, Guildford and King's Lynn

Contents

Figures and tables

FIGURES

TABLES

Acknowledgements

Many friends and economists have been helpful in providing examples and suggesting solutions in this book. We would like to thank Steve Landsberg, University of Rochester; Mark Perry, Jacksonville University; Paul Heyne, University of Washington; Roger LeRoy Miller, University of Texas, Arlington; Larry T. Wimmer and Royal Skousen, Brigham Young University; Roger Garrison, Auburn University; Robert Higgs, The Independent Institute; Harry Kypraios and Eric Schutz, Rollins College. We are indebted to Sharon Miller for kindly, swiftly, and efficiently accommodating our belated request for a word processing conversion, and for Chris Kahl's rapid and reliable work in locating and obtaining needed references. Lastly, we would like to thank each other, our co-authors, who made numerous suggestions for changes, most of which we readily accepted.

Preface

Why are the best Washington apples primarily available outside the state of Washington? Why does a dinner that sells for $20 cost only $10 at lunch? Why do supermarkets often charge more per unit for large sizes than smaller sizes of peanut butter, tuna fish and catsup? Why is good economic news often bad news on Wall Street? Intriguing puzzles and paradoxes like these pervade our economic lives. Are there principles and tools that can enable us better to understand and even resolve them? The authors' affirmative answer is what motivated this book.

This project developed out of two different sets of interests in puzzles and paradoxes. Mark Skousen had wanted to do a book on puzzles and paradoxes that economists have dealt with in the past and those that we now encounter in our earning, consuming and investing activities; such paradoxes can be resolved with careful thinking about economics. Kenna Taylor had also been interested in doing a book on puzzles and paradoxes that mainstream economic theory had difficulty resolving. When Mark first suggested co-authoring a book four years ago under that title, our different interests in the project did not lead us to a quick consensus, and we moved on to other endeavours. Early in 1995 Mark raised the issue again, and we decided to co-author a project that would satisfy our mutual interests.

We agreed to address three kinds of puzzles and paradoxes. The first type derives from the everyday observance of phenomena that seem to belie common sense or a lay understanding of economics. These can usually be resolved by the careful application of basic economic principles such as an undergraduate student of economics would acquire. A second type of puzzle or paradox is an empirical phenomenon or theoretical idea that perplexed economists in the past but which has been resolved, in the process advancing economic theory. A third type refers to empirical or conceptual anomalies that remain unresolved and present a challenge to economic theory.

Because of the plethora of each kind of economic puzzle and paradox, we made no attempt to be comprehensive, though we did try to select ones that would be representative of economics as a whole. Generally, we each followed our own interests and developed the puzzle or paradox cases of concern to us. Although we have initialled each case to indicate authorship, all cases have been reviewed and critiqued by the other author. While we have attempted to be judicious in addressing each case, our solutions are undoubtedly shaped by our belief systems. Applying labels intended to organize a body of thought to the ideas of an individual can be misleading. Bearing this in mind we are willing to say that Mark Skousen uses a free-market perspective tempered by a concern for empirical evidence. Kenna Taylor uses a neo-institutionalist perspective, broadly defined. Both authors share a strong orientation toward understanding human behaviour within a rationality framework. We stress the role of incentives, especially material incentives, in motivating behaviour. We are also drawn to approaches to understanding economic puzzles and paradoxes that allow for less than instantaneous individual and market adjustment for a variety of reasons including ignorance, uncertainty, and adjustment costs.

Students of economics, lay persons, and other social scientists should find this book a fruitful way to see how economics has been and is used to resolve theoretical problems and empirical issues. While economists will be familiar with many of the puzzles and paradoxes, they should find some that they have not considered and others that are addressed in interesting ways. We hope they will find them a useful source of information for both teaching and research.

Our format has been to present each puzzle or paradox, indicate its history and resolve it as succinctly as possible. The central economic concepts employed are indicated and a brief bibliography is included, should the reader wish to explore the topic further. We hope that these cases will stimulate further thought about these ideas, and we welcome any comments, critiques and suggestions. If interest indicates, we would expand our coverage of these and other paradoxes and puzzles in a subsequent work, including contributions from others. Our addresses are given below:

Mark Skousen; e-mail: mskousen@aol.com
Kenna Taylor; e-mail: ktaylor@rollins.edu
Economics Department, Rollins College, Winter Park, FL 32789

Introduction

An economic puzzle is a phenomenon not well explained by the use of simple economic principles, but which, when economic theory is carefully applied or expanded, can be understood in an appealing way. An economic paradox is a phenomenon that seems to be contradictory by received opinion or common sense, but which can be resolved with economic theory.

Economic theory usually begins from the premise that individual behaviour is rational. This is assumed, not proven, so it has the status of a basic behavioural belief. Two conceptions of rationality are used to generate the central concepts of economics. Core rationality formally assumes that an individual has preferences which are complete and transitive. This results in consistent behaviour, the desired goal. More informally, core rationality depicts individual preferences as fully formed (that is, all relevant options are considered and clearly understood), stable (that is, 'tastes' are fixed), and reflected in the actual choices made. Economic rationality includes core rationality and two motivational assumptions: that individuals are materially driven and that they are egoistic. Materially driven behaviour means that an individual's actions are dominated by the desire to acquire goods: the individual prefers more to less and values the goods themselves, not the process of acquiring them. Egoism implies that the pursuit of self-interest is the dominant motive, and that human values are all that matter. Most traditional economic analyses assume economic rationality, but core rationality is employed when the economic approach is used to examine behaviour not thought to be mostly materialistic (such as political behaviour) or egoistic (such as family behaviour).

Central economic concepts are key principles that follow from core or economic rationality. These make up a theoretical tool kit and some combination of them is always needed in resolving puzzles and paradoxes in economics. The rest stand ready to provide another dimension to a solution. Central economic concepts need to be combined with auxiliary information relevant to the specific problem. Auxiliary information includes empirical data and key economic ideas that are developed out of the central concepts. Our list of central economic concepts would include the following:

1

- Property rights. These are rights to acquire, utilize, and transfer things of real value, and their enforcement is needed to motivate the economic behaviour that forms well-functioning markets.
- Supply and demand. The interaction of buyers and sellers creates markets, the impetus of surpluses and shortages coordinating production and desire for goods and inputs. Supply and demand mutually determine the quantity and price revealed in the market such that no buyers or sellers remain unsatisfied at these market prices.
- Diminishing marginal returns. An input applied to a production process will increase output, but, after some point, the additions to output will become progressively less if at least one other input is fixed in amount. This produces a direct price and quantity supply relation.
- Diminishing marginal utility. As more of a good is consumed, the total utility of consuming a good always increases, but, as more urgent wants are satisfied first, the extra satisfaction received from an additional unit of the good becomes less and less.
- Substitution. Substitutes in demand and supply exist for virtually all goods and inputs. A higher price for a given good or input elicits buyers to substitute another and sellers to substitute it for others. Substitution generates an inverse price and quantity demand relation.
- Price/income relation. Any change in the price of a good consumed by a buyer produces both an income and quantity change in the opposite direction for the buyer. When aggregate prices change, aggregate income also moves in the opposite direction.
- Markets and information. Markets access and develop information needed by market participants to coordinate buying and selling decisions, and this is reflected in levels and changes in prices.
- Marginal analysis. When decisions are made, the benefits and costs to people take place at the margins of decision making. Decisions are unaffected by sunk costs and benefits previously gained.
- Scarcity and opportunity cost. Scarcity makes choice inevitable, and the value of any choice is the value of the next best choice forgone.
- Rational expectations. Individuals look at current, past and anticipated future variables before making a current decision.
- Time preference. Individuals in general have a preference for

goods now instead of later and demand compensation to postpone consumption.

- Voluntary exchange and surplus. Voluntary exchange by all buyers and sellers generates a price that, for the combined units exchanged, does not reveal the maximum that buyers are willing to pay for a good; nor does it reveal the minimum that sellers are willing to sell the good for. Consequently, consumer and producer surplus accompanies such exchanges.
- Subjectiveness of demand. An individual's demand for a good is inherently subjective and introspective so objective characteristics of a good cannot be used to infer the perceived quality of a good.
- Direct and indirect effects. Changes in economic variables have direct effects on human behaviour, but these direct effects lead to further indirect and delayed changes that may either exacerbate or retard the earlier direct effects.

The 44 puzzles and paradoxes to follow utilize a rationality concept and many of the above central concepts, along with auxiliary information. Each case lists a rationality conception if it is a focus, and the relevant central concepts and other economic ideas that have been used to understand and resolve the puzzle or paradox. Not all cases have been resolved, and there may be other ways to resolve them than those herein. For convenience we have categorized the cases as primarily microeconomic or macroeconomic. Microeconomic cases include 1–25. Macroeconomic cases include 26–44.

Cases and concepts

1. THE ADAM SMITH PARADOX

In 1776 in *The Wealth of Nations*, Adam Smith asserted that when people try to gain more for themselves materially and are not impeded from doing so, they collectively end up benefiting society even though that was not their intent. How can this be?

Central Concepts and Key Economic Ideas

- Economic rationality
- Supply and demand
- Market failures
- Economic incentives
- Economic efficiency
- General equilibrium

2. THE DIAMOND–WATER PARADOX

'Diamonds are expensive, but they have little practical value; water is cheap, but it has great practical value.' How do you explain this paradox that plagued Adam Smith and other classical economists?

Central Concepts and Key Economic Ideas

- Voluntary exchange and surplus
- Marginal analysis
- Diminishing marginal utility
- Scarcity and opportunity cost
- Production for use versus production for profit

3. THE WATER PROBLEM

'People cannot live without water. No one will reduce his use of water just because the price goes up. Therefore, it will do no good for the utility company to raise the price of water during a water shortage. Water must be rationed.' Are absolute necessities like water exempt from the laws of supply and demand?

Central Concepts and Key Economic Ideas

- Diminishing marginal returns
- Supply and demand
- Demand elasticity
- Privatization

4. THE CASE OF THE FOURTH EGG

The law of declining marginal utility states that each additional good provides less benefit to the user. But suppose it takes four eggs to bake a cake. In that case, the marginal utility of the first, second and third egg has much less value than the fourth egg, because with the fourth egg, you can now make a cake. The fourth egg has greater utility than the first three because without it a cake cannot be produced properly. How can you square this situation with the law of declining marginal utility?

Central Concepts and Key Economic Ideas

- Diminishing marginal utility
- Homogeneity of goods

5. PROFITING FROM PANTS

Terry's Threads prices the popular Panther pants at $20 a pair and sells 1000 pairs. Clara's Clothier in the same area sets the price at $30 a pair and sells 600 pairs. Who is the more perceptive purveyor of Panther pants?

Central Concepts and Key Economic Ideas

- Supply and demand
- Marginal analysis
- Profit maximization

6. THE PRICE OF QUALITY

Bogg Downe wants to buy a car and budgetary concerns have prompted him to consider the used car market. Not knowing much about the used car market Bogg sought the advice of several friends. Wanda Most told him to look at the price as an indicator of quality because 'you always get what you pay for'. Penny Pincher told him to 'shop for the least expensive car you desire'. Wylie Deals told him 'when you buy a used car you buy somebody's problem'. Whose advice should Bogg take?

Central Concepts and Key Economic Ideas

- Supply and demand
- Subjectiveness of demand
- Markets and information
- Uncertainty and economic institutions

7. THE RATIONALITY AND RISK PUZZLE

Ernest Workman is a financially conservative worker earning $35 000 annually. He has his savings of $10 000 in certificates of deposit at a local bank, and his monthly investment of $200 is divided between well-established bond and blue-chip stock funds. Yet, once or twice a week Ernest spends $10 playing the lottery and makes a once-a-year trip to Biloxi with $1000 to gamble, a trip from which he almost always comes home with little or no cash. Does Ernest, like many others, combine conservative with risky behaviour because he lacks discipline or the education to do otherwise? Or is he simply irrational?

Central Concepts and Key Economic Ideas

- Economic rationality
- Scarcity and opportunity cost
- Diminishing marginal utility

- Risk and reward

8. GOLD'S BACKWARD SUPPLY CURVE

In the 1970s, gold prices skyrocketed while mining companies reduced their gold output. The production of gold actually declined during the 1970s, then increased substantially in the 1980s – when the price of gold fell. What was the rationale for this behaviour?

Central Concepts and Key Economic Ideas

- Direct and indirect effects
- Backward-bending supply curve

9. THE POSITIVE SLOPING DEMAND CURVE?

The law of demand states that if you raise the price of a product, people buy less of it. Publisher Image Creator prints up a thousand copies of an investment report, which they sell for $10 each. Only a handful are sold. Mr Creator decides to redesign the essay into a special 'executive' report and raise the price to $100 for this 'unique' product. Amazingly, the publisher sells out the entire stock. Has Creator discovered a loop-hole in the law of a downward-sloping demand curve?

Central Concepts and Key Economic Ideas

- Subjectiveness of demand
- Marketing and information
- Demand elasticity
- Taste change

10. THE LEISURE PARADOX

According to the law of supply for labour, the higher the wages the more people are willing to work. Tim Toil earns $10 an hour and works a 40-hour workweek plus an average 10 hours a week in overtime. He gets a rise to $15 an hour, and decides to stop working overtime and spend more time with his family. Does Tim's decision in favour of leisure violate the law of supply for labour?

Central Concepts and Key Economic Ideas

- Substitution
- Scarcity and opportunity cost
- Backward-bending supply curve for labour

11.   THE PRICE DISCRIMINATION DILEMMA

Seniors and children pay $3 for the same movie that others pay $6 to see. Virtually the same meal that costs $16 during the evening at Gary's Gourmet costs $9 if one comes between 5:00 and 6:00 p.m. for the 'early bird special'. The practice of charging different prices to different individuals for the same good is called price discrimination. It implies the existence of monopoly power and so is economically inefficient, and it is often illegal. Yet not only is price discrimination pervasive in society, it is an important way in which society covertly and unintendedly redistributes consumption, much of it from the rich to the poor. How?

Central Concepts and Key Economic Ideas

- Voluntary exchange and surplus
- Marginal analysis
- Price discrimination and monopoly power
- Redistribution
- Demand elasticity

12.   A HOT VACATION SPOT

The Wall Street Journal (21 July 1995) reported that 'occupancy at Phoenix-area resorts stands well above 70 percent this summer, up from barely 50 percent three years ago'. The article offered the view that an important cause of this increase was the rise in hotel room rates. Does this violate the law of demand?

Central Concepts and Key Economic Ideas

- Markets and information
- Subjectiveness of demand
- Taste changes

13. THE RARE CASE OF A GIFFEN GOOD?

During the Irish famine of the 1840s, the price of potatoes skyrocketed, but the poor ate less meat and *more* potatoes! So claimed Sir Robert Giffen, who was allegedly the first to observe this phenomenon. How can you explain the existence of a Giffen good, which appears to contradict the law of demand?

Central Concepts and Key Economic Ideas

- Substitution
- Price–income relations
- Indifference curve analysis
- Inferior goods

14. THE CASE OF THE COSTLY CATSUP

Why do supermarket items such as peanut butter, tuna fish and catsup often sell for more per ounce in larger sizes as compared to smaller sizes? Is this a violation of the law of downward-sloping demand?

Central Concepts and Key Economic Ideas

- Supply and demand
- Voluntary exchange and surplus
- Price discrimination

15. THE MAIL ORDER QUESTION

A mail order publisher tests two prices for the same book, $15 and $25. He mails each ad to 5000 randomly selected names from a list of book buyers. One hundred people order the book for $25, resulting in gross revenues of $2500, while 200 people respond to the $15 offer, with gross revenues of $3000. The mail order publisher decides to advertise all future books for $25. Did he make a mistake?

Central Concepts and Key Economic Ideas

- Markets and information
- Profit maximization

- Costs and revenues

16.   THE BUSINESSMAN'S QUERY

'An upward-sloping supply curve doesn't make sense in my business. All I know is that if I raise my prices, revenues don't go up, they go down. I don't sell more products, I sell less.' Can you straighten out this businessman's thinking?

Central Concepts and Key Economic Ideas

- Supply and demand
- Demand elasticity
- Profit maximization

17.   ARE TEACHERS UNDERPAID?

Outstanding athletes such as Michael Jordan and Wayne Gretsky and famous movie stars and entertainers such as John Travolta and Garth Brooks earn multimillion-dollar annual incomes while the very best teachers earn considerably less. Were a survey to be taken most people would surely agree with the proposition that 'education is more important than entertainment'. Are teachers underpaid?

Central Concepts and Key Economic Ideas

- Markets and information
- Supply and demand
- Social values and market prices
- Derived demand

18.   THE POLLUTION PUZZLE

A 'good' is something we desire to have while a 'bad' is something we want to get rid of. Pollution is a bad. Since pollution is a bad by definition, logic implies that we should eliminate it. Why don't we?

Central Concepts and Key Economic Ideas

- Diminishing marginal returns
- Diminishing marginal utility
- Goods and bads
- Biology and economics
- Negative externalities

19. ARE MARKET WAGES FAIR?

In a market, the wages a person earns tend to reflect that person's productivity. More work effort implies greater worker productivity and this in turn implies higher worker wages. Economic systems that do not constrain this process have higher income inequality than systems that constrain it. Is this then a fair way to determine wages?

Central Concepts and Key Economic Ideas

- Supply and demand
- Marginal analysis
- Choice and productivity
- Markets and economic institutions

20. THE HIGHLY VALUED OCCUPATION NOBODY WANTS

A survey of college students found that farming was ranked the number one most important occupation in the world. Yet less than 1 per cent of the students wanted to be farmers. How do you explain this apparently irrational response?

Central Concepts and Key Economic Ideas

- Diminishing marginal utility
- Marginal productivity of labour
- Engel's law

21. THE STOCK MARKET PUZZLER

Louis Bachelier, a French mathematician and stock market observer, wrote in his 1900 dissertation, 'Theory of speculation': 'It seems that the market, the aggregate of speculators, *at a given instant* can believe in neither a market rise nor a market fall, since, for each quoted price, there are as many buyers as sellers' (original emphasis).* Therefore, according to Bachelier's logic, the stock market can never rise or fall, but must stand still. How do you explain why the stock market moves, sometimes dramatically, given that for every buyer there is a willing seller?

Central Concepts and Key Economic Ideas

- Supply and demand
- Efficiency
- Stock market theories

22. APPLES AND THE ALCHIAN–ALLEN THEOREM

In Washington state, it is casually observed that the best Washington delicious apples are exported out of the state. This contradicts common sense. Shouldn't the best apples be found where they are produced?

Central Concepts and Key Economic Ideas

- Scarcity and opportunity cost
- Alchian–Allen theorem
- Fixed vs variable costs
- Tax theory

23. THE PERFECT-MARKET PUZZLE

In perfect financial markets, the prices of the assets are information-rich, so that it is virtually impossible for any individual consistently to buy and sell a stock at a greater profit than the market average. The US financial market is often considered the best example of a perfect

* Peter L. Bernstein, *Capital Ideas: The Improbable Origins of Modern Wall Street*, New York: Free Press, 1992, p. 20.

market. Yet millions of investors in the US financial market (and world markets) continually try to beat the market averages. Are financial markets very imperfect or are people very irrational?

Central Concepts and Key Economic Ideas

- Supply and demand
- Markets and information
- Market noise
- Economic theory and evidence
- Principal–agent problem

24. THE STARVATION OF BURIDAN'S ASS

A hungry donkey faces two equally attractive stacks of hay. He is simply unable to decide which hay stack to go to. As a result, he starves. What's wrong with this case of indifference?

Central Concepts and Key Economic Ideas

- Core rationality
- Scarcity and opportunity cost
- Indifference curve analysis

25. DOES STUDYING ECONOMICS MAKE ONE IMMORAL?

Mainstream economic models are built upon the assumption that economic agents are economically rational. This behaviour is presumed to lead to societal well-being. However, many have argued that the adoption of this approach to understanding human behaviour creates a deep scepticism or even cynicism about human nature, leaving no room for belief in spontaneity, spirituality, and altruism as important parts of the human character. Furthermore, it promotes the adoption of this behaviour even when it is not socially beneficent. If so, an approach that is justified by its beneficent social consequences ends up producing morally inferior people. Can we resolve this dilemma?

Central Concepts and Key Economic Ideas

- Property rights
- Economic rationality
- Economic values
- Market failures

26. THE SAVERS' DILEMMA

The public's desire to increase the saving rate expands the supply of saving, which reduces the interest rate paid on savings accounts. As a result, people are discouraged from saving and decide to save less. Therefore, it is impossible to change the saving rate. Correct?

Central Concepts and Key Economic Ideas

- Direct and indirect effects
- Supply and demand
- Saving and investment

27. KEYNES'S BANANA PLANTATION

What would happen if a community that only produces bananas decides to save more? The same number of bananas is produced, but people spend less money on bananas. Prices fall, profits turn to losses, workers are laid off, income drops, and even fewer bananas are sold. Eventually, the community starves to death. How can you resolve Keynes's dilemma?

Central Concepts and Key Economic Ideas

- Direct and indirect effects
- Interest rates
- Saving and investing
- Anti-saving theory

28. PRODUCING CARS THAT DON'T SELL

In a *Forbes* column (6 August 1990), economist Alan Reynolds asks, 'Does it make sense for people to buy fewer cars so that manufacturers can build more auto factories?' How do you respond to this criticism of savings?

Central Concepts and Key Economic Ideas

- Time preference
- Technology
- Interest rates
- Anti-saving theory

29. THE FECKLESS FORECAST AND POLICY PURVEYOR PUZZLE

'GDP will grow by 1–2 per cent next year, and inflation will be in the 3–4 per cent range.' The kind of forecast is continually being made by business economists. 'To regain our eroding living standards we must become internationally competitive.' Such policy pronouncements are regularly made in the media by economists. Yet such forecasts are frequently wrong, and these policy statements are frequently misguided. They both often overstate the extent of knowledge we have about the economy. This undermines the credibility of economics and economic analysis. Yet it persists. Why?

Central Concepts and Key Economic Ideas

- Economic rationality
- Economic theory and empiricism
- Market and non-market values

30. THE GROWING BUT DECLINING GAP PUZZLE

The income gap between rich and poor countries is growing at the same time that poor countries are gaining on the rich. How can this be so? What does this mean for the future of the poor?

Central Concepts and Key Economic Ideas

- Levels and rates of change of variables
- Cross-sections and time series
- Compound growth

31. THE PERPETUAL POVERTY PUZZLE

In is 1964 State of the Union address President Lyndon Johnson declared a 'War on Poverty' to eliminate poverty in the USA and create economic self-sufficiency. Since then the federal government has devoted billions of dollars to doing so. The policy has failed and poverty, by some measures, has actually become worse over the past 20 years. Why cannot the wealthiest country in world history put an end to poverty, or even reduce it significantly?

Central Concepts and Key Economic Ideas

- Economic rationality
- Direct and indirect effects
- Scarcity and opportunity cost
- Economic incentives

32. THE PARADOX OF THRIFT

The classic textbook case, where greater thriftiness reduces spending, forces business to cut back production, which in turns lays off workers, reduces income and ultimately reduces saving. 'While savings may pave the road to riches for an individual, if the nation as a whole decides to save more, the result may be a recession and poverty for all' (Baumol and Blinder, 1988: 192). How can the paradox of thrift be resolved?

Central Concepts and Key Economic Ideas

- Direct and indirect effects
- Saving and investing
- Interest rates
- Business and consumer expectations

33. THE GOLD ABSURDITY

Paul Samuelson declares, 'How absurd to waste resources digging gold out of the bowels of the earth, only to inter it back again in the vaults of Fort Knox, Kentucky!'* How can this apparent absurdity under a gold standard be rationalized?

Central Concepts and Key Economic Ideas

- Direct and indirect effects
- Efficiency
- Monetary systems

34. THE WAGER OVER WAGES

In 1914, Henry Ford tripled the averge wage at his auto factory to $5 a day. Ford hired new workers and productivity and profits both increased substantially. In 1930, Ford raised wages (in real terms), but profits fell, and Ford had to lay off workers. How can you explain this difference in outcome?

Central Concepts and Key Economic Ideas

- Economic rationality
- Direct and indirect effects
- Labour productivity
- Theory of wages
- Keynesianism
- Business cycles

35. THE VOTING BEHAVIOUR PUZZLE

Since the probability of influencing an election by one's vote is virtually nil, and the cost of gaining useful information about the candidates is quite high, the act of voting seems to be irrational. Yet millions of people, some of them of obvious intelligence, and some of them well informed, do vote in national, state and local elections. How can we explain this puzzle?

* Paul A. Samuelson, *Economics*, 7th edn, New York: McGraw-Hill, 1976, p. 700.

Central Concepts and Key Economic Ideas

- Core and economic rationality
- Rational expectations
- Public interest and public choice theory
- Rational ignorance

36. THE VOTING PARADOX

In 1951 Kenneth Arrow (1921–), who won a Nobel Prize in economics in 1972, showed that, with a desirable set of assumptions about human preferences, there was no voting institution, including majority voting, that could guarantee a consistent set of outcomes. In other words the basis of democracy was irrational. How can this paradox be solved?

Central Concepts and Key Economic Ideas

- Core and economic rationality
- Rational expectations
- Economic and political behaviour

37. A TAXING DEBATE

Argument A: 'To reduce the federal deficit, taxes should be raised. An increase in taxes will cut the deficit, reduce interest rates and stimulate the economy.'
Argument B: 'To reduce the federal deficit, taxes should be cut. A tax cut will stimulate economic activity, expand the tax base, and increase government revenues, which will reduce the deficit.'
Which argument should prevail?

Central Concepts and Key Economic Ideas

- Direct and indirect effects
- Supply-side economics
- Tax policy
- Deficit spending
- Laffer curve

38. THE BLESSINGS OF DESTRUCTION

Frederic Bastiat (1801–50) considers the case of a young hoodlum who throws a brick through a window of a baker's shop. This act of violence creates business to replace the window. Therefore, is not the hoodlum a public benefactor rather than a menace to society?

Central Concepts and Key Economic Ideas

- Direct and indirect effects
- Cost–benefit analysis
- War economics

39. THE INTEREST RATE DILEMMA

Argument A: 'Higher interest rates are good for the economy because it means higher income for retirees invested in money market funds and Treasury bills. This additional income will stimulate the economy.'
Argument B: 'Higher interest rates are bad for the economy because it means borrowing money is more expensive and will therefore hurt business and consumer spending.'
Which argument is correct? Are higher interest rates good or bad for the economy?

Central Concepts and Key Economic Ideas

- Direct and indirect effects
- Scarcity and opportunity cost
- Theory of interest rates
- Savings and debt

40. THE POPULATION PUZZLER

If a married couple has two children, the chance of having a boy and a girl is 50 per cent. If they have four children, the chance of having two boys and two girls is ... only 37.5 per cent (six out of 16 possibilities). If they have eight kids, the chance of having four boys and four girls is 27.3 per cent. In other words, as the world is populated more and more, there is less and less chance of having an equal number of boys and girls.

Yet historically large populations are approximately 50–50 male–female. How do you reconcile this contradiction?

Central Concepts and Key Economic Ideas

- Population theory

41. THE EFFICIENCY VERSUS EQUALITY PUZZLE

The economic virtue of the market system resides in its ability to produce more than a non-market system of what people want in a society. Yet there is no guarantee that everyone will participate in the overall benefit to society of a market system. Indeed, the USA, the most market-oriented industrial country in the world, also has one of the most unequal income distributions of any of the industrial countries. Does more efficient production invariably imply more unequally distributed income?

Central Concepts and Key Economic Ideas

- Economic rationality
- Economic efficiency
- Income distribution
- Equality of opportunity and equality of outcomes

42. THE NATIONAL DEBT: ASSET OR LIABILITY?

Economist Robert Eisner states, 'The greater a person's debt, given his assets, the less his net worth; the greater the Government's debt, the greater the people's net worth' (Eisner, *New York Times*, 19 March 1994). How is this possible?

Central Concepts and Key Economic Ideas

- Direct and indirect effects
- Scarcity and opportunity cost
- Interest rates and bond market
- Inflation
- Crowding out

43.   THE LEONTIEF PARADOX

The Heckscher–Ohlin or factor proportions theory, the dominant approach to comparative advantage in international trade, says that a country will specialize in and export those goods using its most abundant factor most intensively. In the 1950s it was clear that the USA was more capital-abundant than any other country. Yet when Wassily Leontief looked at the evidence, he found that the USA was exporting labour-intensive goods. How is this possible?

Central Concepts and Key Economic Ideas

- Supply and demand
- General equilibrium
- Economic theory and evidence
- Comparative advantage

44.   THE PERVERSITY OF WALL STREET

'Strong employment gains tend to be negative for both stocks and bonds', states Marty Zweig, a Wall Street wizard (*The Zweig Forecast*, 29 July 1994). 'A robust economy could hurt stocks', reports *The Wall Street Journal*. 'That's because a robust economy probably would drive up short-term interest rates, causing investors to dump stocks in favor of the improving yields on safer, fixed-income investments' (*Wall Street Journal*, 13 December 1993, C1). Yet stock prices are ultimately determined by earnings and profits, which in turn suggest a robust economy. How do you explain this perversity of Wall Street?

Central Concepts and Key Economic Ideas

- Economic rationality
- Direct and indirect effects
- Monetary policy
- Interest rates and bond market
- Growth theory

1. The Adam Smith paradox

In 1776 in The Wealth of Nations, *Adam Smith asserted that when people try to gain more for themselves materially and are not impeded from doing so, they collectively end up benefiting society even though that was not their intent. How can this be?*

This was an important issue addressed by Adam Smith (1723–90) in *The Wealth of Nations*. Adam Smith stated that an individual producer ' . . . intends only his own gain, and he is in this, as in many other cases, led by an invisible hand to promote an end which was no part of his intention' (Smith, 1937: 423). The Adam Smith paradox has always been the core paradox of economics, motivating its development for over 200 years. Its validity continues to be challenged by religious authorities, academic thinkers outside economics, and economists themselves. Nonetheless, human behaviour legitimized by the invisible hand paradox has increasingly guided economic and political life in Western and even non-Western nations in the twentieth century. Furthermore, Smith's more general insight that an overall outcome may be different from the intentions of the individuals who create the outcome has been called by the Nobel prize-winning economist Kenneth Arrow ' . . . the most important intellectual contribution that economic thought has made to the general understanding of social processes' (Arrow, 1968: 376). Is this important intellectual idea sound?

Adam Smith, along with the other thinkers of the Enlightenment (late seventeenth to late eighteenth century) sought to liberate people from both church dogma (Heilbroner, 1986: 2) and the many passions such as pride and envy (Holmes, 1990) that historically shaped human affairs. Church doctrine promoted the lack of incentive for temporal improvements in the human condition through its emphasis on self-denial and the supreme importance of the afterlife relative to worldly life. The clergy tended to see the average person as base and inferior, ruled by passions which needed to be constrained. Church doctrine also supported an aristocracy whose temperament, Smith believed, was not conducive to engaging in commercial activity. The passions which worried the clergy and others included, besides pride and envy, anger and the desire for glory or revenge. Their concerns were well based,

for historically such passions had led to battles and wars that under-
mined political and economic stability. Commercial activity had been
vilified by the clergy and intellectuals since the Middle Ages as being
motivated by base human instincts, and this attitude carried over during
the creation of the nation states in Europe. Greed and avarice were
controlled by a set of strong rules and regulations by government known
as mercantilism. Smith's emphasis on the socially beneficent effects of
material self-interest was an assault on the idea that societies be guided
by both clerical asceticism and the belief that socially destructive passions had to be kept in check by rule, regulations and the strong
involvement of governments. Instead, Smith argued that there is a
propensity for humans to ' ... truck, barter, and exchange one thing
for another' (Smith, 1937: 13). This propensity was to be circumscribed
within the laws and mores of society, which represented the individual
virtues of justice and prudence (Brown, 1991: 212–16).

Smith thus sought to socially legitimize a behaviour that had been
excoriated because in its system-wide effects he saw an order or
harmony where others saw only chaos. Smith used the 'invisible hand'
to explain how individuals' rational calculation of their material self-
interest will lead to competition which in turn will produce high output
and incomes for the whole economic system and create material wealth
for society. Smith saw this self-regulating process as a 'natural law' that
God had created for social harmony. It should be discovered by humans
and should substitute for the rules and regulations of mercantilism. In
short, Smith sought to find a universal natural law for economics that
would replace the human law that had guided thinking about economics
since the Middle Ages (Screpanti and Zamagni, 1993: 17, 54). He
believed that government commercial policy retarded the changes
needed to produce material well-being for the whole society. Self-
interest could be relied on because everyone was assumed to have a
good measure of it, and, even though Smith acknowledged the importance of a variety of motivations in humans, he believed that material
self-interest was dominant enough to produce social harmony.

However, the fact that material self-interest was but one among many
motivations creates a problem for Smith's analysis of the invisible hand.
How can we be sure that at any point in the set of exchange relations
that make up the invisible hand, it is material self-interest and not some
other motive that will dominate? This was a problem for Smith because
he did not distinguish between total utility and marginal utility. The
neoclassical economists who came later did so.

Thus a variety of motives make up the psyche of each individual and
comprise total utility, but that need not determine the value of goods

exchanged since it is marginal utility that motivates exchange. Why should the marginal utility of exchange be guided by self-interest exclusively or at least predominantly? Because the context of exchange makes it so. At the time we contemplate buying or selling a good, we have narrowed our choices to those that serve the same purpose, often non-material and non-egoistic in nature. Decisions such as buying a toy for a child for love or buying a new sports car for pride or envy of a neighbour's car are clearly rooted in motivations other than materialistic ones, but in the context of picking a product that will satisfy these motivations, it will be material concerns (price, quality, quantity, one's income) that will dominate the particular choice. So long as material self-interest determines behaviour at the time of the exchange decision, other motivations do not matter. While Smith produced many examples of the beneficent effects of free exchange and the rudiments of the logic of it, it still remained to be shown more rigorously that this methodological individualism could generate a full and rigorously consistent account of how the overall material well-being of a society was enhanced by such a system.

It was not until the first part of the twentieth century that Alfred Marshall (1842–1924) provided the theoretical elements of supply, demand, and mutual causation needed for a resolution of the invisible hand paradox. Today Smith's social harmony is referred to as the first fundamental theorem of welfare economics – that competition in a market system allocates resources efficiently. Also called Pareto optimality, with reference to the Italian economist, Vilfredo Pareto (1848–1923), efficiency means that after all trade takes place and productive methods are chosen, no one can be made better off without someone else being made worse off. The problem with this resolution is that it depends on a number of unrealistic assumptions. Pareto optimality assumes that property rights are fully specified and enforced, only private goods are produced, no externalities exist, no informational asymmetries exist, and existing income and wealth distribution is accepted as equitable.

In general none of these conditions hold in reality, and this gives rise to a variety of problems that tend to negate the efficiency outcome of competitive markets. These so-called market failures include free-rider behaviour (with externalities and public goods); moral hazards, adverse selection, job signalling and principal–agent problems (with asymmetric information); and rent-seeking behaviour (with inequitable income and wealth distribution). There are two conceptual solutions to these problems. One is to argue that the market system should be buttressed with appropriate government actions (changes in full property rights), so that public goods can be provided, externalities can be internalized by market participants, informational asymmetries can be eliminated, and unacceptable income and wealth inequalities can be corrected. A second solution is to allow economic theory to embody a richer array of motives than material self-interest alone, particularly the desire for social inter-action and a sense of community. Neither of these solutions has been intellectually satisfying. By allowing more government or a broader range of human motivations, the intellectual basis for the Adam Smith paradox is dissolved. That is, if people care about others and are regu-larly public-spirited, and if government is needed to achieve efficiency and social harmony anyway, there is no paradox to resolve.

Another strand of thought has addressed the Adam Smith paradox more formally. Beginning in the nineteenth century Leon Walras (1834–1910) introduced general equilibrium theory. General equilib-rium theory is an abstract and formal approach to deriving Smith's social harmony. It is motivated by methodological individualism and traces out the interrelations among all input and output markets to find an equilibrium that results in an efficient allocation of resources. The key problems addressed by this approach have been to prove that such an equilibrium exists, that it is unique, and that it is stable, all of which are needed for the resolution of the Adam Smith paradox. In the 1950s the proof of the existence of a general equilibrium with optimality properties was achieved (Arrow and Debreu, 1954). However, neither the stability of a general equilibrium nor the uniqueness of general equilibrium was proven nor is thought to be provable at this time. What does this mean? Only that individual behaviour is not sufficient to produce a unique or stable equilibrium. The 'invisible hand' cannot be achieved solely by rational, materially driven, egoistic behaviour (Screpanti and Zamagni, 1993: 340–55). One way to resolve the Adam Smith paradox is to abandon the strong version of methodological individualism – that only individual behaviour matters. This done, social values and institutions (including government) are allowed to affect human behaviour in economic models. Whether or not this produces an optimum is undetermined. This approach would move economic theory away from methodological individualism and the emphasis on *laissez-faire* in order to guarantee the economic well-being of a nation. Again, the Adam Smith paradox is dissolved, not resolved.

K.C.T.

REFERENCES

Arrow, Kenneth (1968), 'Economic Equilibrium', in D.L. Sills (ed.), *International Encyclopedia of the Social Sciences*, **4**, New York: Macmillan and Free Press.

Arrow, Kenneth and Gerard Debreu (1954), 'Existence of an equilibrium for a Competitive Economy', *Econometrica*, **22**, 265–90.

Brown, Vivienne (1991), 'Signifying Voices – Reading the "Adam Smith Problem" ', *Economics and Philosophy*, **7**, 187–220.

Heilbroner, Robert L. (ed.) (1986), *The Essential Adam Smith*, New York: W.W. Norton.

Holmes, Stephen (1990), 'The Secret History of Self Interest', in Jane J. Mansbridge (ed.), *Beyond Self Interest*, Chicago, Illinois: University of Chicago Press.

Screpanti, Ernesto and Stefano Zamagni (1993), *An Outline of the History of Economic Thought*, Oxford: Clarendon Press.

Smith, Adam (1937 [1776]), *An Inquiry into the Nature and Causes of The Wealth of Nations*, New York: Modern Library.

2. The diamond–water paradox

'Diamonds are expensive, but they have little practical value; water is cheap, but it has great practical value.' How do you explain this paradox that plagued Adam Smith and other classical economists?

Adam Smith (1729–90) raised the famous paradox of value in Chapter 4 of Book I of *The Wealth of Nations*: 'Nothing is more useful than water: but it will purchase scarce any thing ... A diamond, on the contrary, has scarce any value in use; but a very great quantity of other goods may frequently be had in exchange for it' (Smith, 1937: 28).

Unfortunately, Smith had no ready answer to the paradox. He simply created a strange dichotomy. Water had 'value in use', while diamonds had 'value in exchange'.

Yet, oddly enough, Francis Hutcheson, Smith's former professor, and other scholastic teachers had solved this paradox years earlier. The value and price of a commodity are determined first by subjective consumer demand and then by the relative scarcity or abundance of the good – in short, demand and supply. The more abundant the good, the lower the price; the scarcer the good, the higher the price (Kauder, 1960).

Even more amazing is the fact that Adam Smith resolved the diamond–water paradox in his own lectures, delivered a decade before he wrote his classic *Wealth of Nations*! The difference in price between diamonds and water is one of scarcity. Smith said, 'It is only on account of the plenty of water that it is so cheap as to be got for the lifting, and on account of the scarcity of diamonds ... that they are so dear'. The Scottish professor added that when supply conditions change, the value of a product changes too. Smith noted that a rich merchant lost in the Arabian desert would value water at a very high price. If the quantity of diamonds could 'by industry ... be multiplied,' the price of diamonds would drop significantly (Smith, 1982: 333, 358).

Yet a decade later, when writing *The Wealth of Nations*, his cogent explanation completely vanished, and he was inexplicably unable to resolve the diamond–water paradox. Suddenly Smith separates utility from price. He distinguished between 'value in use' and 'value in exchange', as if nothing connects price and utility. Water had great 'use',

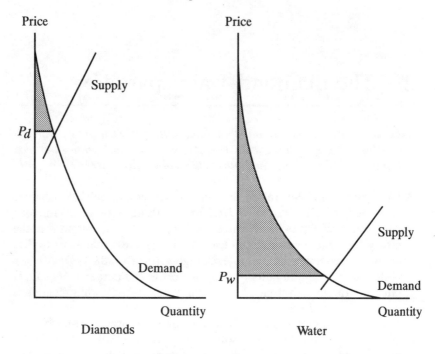

Figure 2.1   Total and marginal utility for diamonds and water

but very little 'value'. A diamond has scarcely any use (this was before diamonds were used in industry), but great 'exchange' value.

In *The Wealth of Nations*, Smith made no mention of the correct solution to this paradox, the relative scarcity of water and diamonds. It was not until the 1870s, a century later, that three economists – Carl Menger, Stanley Jevons and Leon Walras – separately demonstrated that prices (value in exchange) are determined by their marginal utility, not their total utility (value in use). Because water is abundant, an additional unit of water is cheap; because diamonds are extremely scarce, an additional diamond is expensive. Figure 2.1 illustrates how the diamond–water paradox can be resolved. Note that the price is high and total utility (consumer surplus) low for diamonds, while the price is low and total utility (consumer surplus) high for water.

The 1870s marked the beginning of the marginalist revolution, where value is based on marginal utility, but it really marked the restoration of the marginalist tradition that went back to the scholastics and even Aristotle. As Professor Emil Kauder puts it, 'the father of our economic science wrote that water had a great utility and a small value. With these few words Adam Smith had made waste and rubbish out of the thinking of 2,000 years' (Kauder, 1960: 282).

WHY SMITH CHANGED HIS MIND

Why did Adam Smith change his mind between the time he gave his lectures and the publication of *The Wealth of Nations*? It was not due to his absent-mindedness, but perhaps his religious predilections. Smith was a Presbyterian, steeped in Calvinist values. His Calvinist beliefs emphasized the goodness of hard work, useful production, and frugality. *The Wealth of Nations* is full of high-mindedness and virtue. In his mind, diamonds and jewels were vain luxury items and relatively 'useless' compared to water and other 'useful' products, and his economic theory reflected those values.

Readers are frequently baffled by Smith's odd dichotomy between 'productive' and 'unproductive' labour (see the third chapter of Book II in *The Wealth of Nations*). The author refers to the occupations of ministers, physicians, musicians, orators, actors and other producers of services as 'frivolous', while farmers and other producers of goods are 'productive'. Why? Because Smith's Presbyterian conscience argues against consumption in favour of saving and work. As Roger Garrison states, 'The basis for the distinction is not Physiocratic fallacies but Presbyterian values. Productive labour is future oriented; unproductive labour is present oriented' (Garrison, 1985: 290).

But the impact of Smith's artificial dichotomy between value in 'use' and 'exchange' has had a much greater impact than he realized. For it has given ammunition to socialists and other critics of capitalism who complain about the difference in the marketplace between 'production for profit' and 'production for use'. They criticize capitalists for being more interested in 'making profits' than in 'providing a useful service', as if profitable 'exchange' is unrelated to consumer 'use'. Yet clearly they are directly connected. Profitability is a measure of utility, not total use but marginal use, and is the driving force behind the efficient allocation of resources and, hence, maximizes economic growth and a nation's standard of living.

M.S.

REFERENCES

Garrison, Roger (1985), 'West's "Cantillon and Adam Smith": A Comment', *Journal of Libertarian Studies* (Fall).

Kauder, Emil (1960), 'Genesis of the Marginal Utility Theory from Aristotle to the End of the Eighteenth Century', in J. Spengler and W. Allen (eds), *Essays in Economic Thought*, Chicago, Illinois: Rand McNally.

Smith, Adam (1937 [1776]), *The Wealth of Nations*, New York: Modern Library.

Smith, Adam (1982), *Lectures on Jurisprudence*, Indianapolis, Indiana: Liberty Classics.

3. The water problem

'People cannot live without water. No one will reduce his use of water just because the price goes up. Therefore, it will do no good for the utility company to raise the price of water during a water shortage. Water must be rationed.' Are absolute necessities like water exempt from the laws of supply and demand?

The demand for water may be highly inelastic if the supply of water is severely restricted to human survival, but in today's world, the abundance of water is sufficiently large to make demand for it surprisingly elastic. Water consumption varies considerably between cities and is remarkably responsive to price changes.

According to Armen Alchian and William Allen, in 1972 the average per capita daily purchase of water was 230 gallons in Chicago, 150 in New York and Los Angeles, 120 in San Diego and 110 in Boston. 'The quantities reflect, for one thing, differences in industrial use. Chicago has steel- and oil-refining industries, which use a great deal of water; New York City businesses – finance, retail, apparel – are light water users' (Alchian and Allen, 1972: 64–5).

In times of water shortage, could consumption be reduced by raising prices or is physical rationing inevitable? Surprisingly, consumption can be reduced dramatically in a number of ways. Residential and industrial users could use water more efficiently, avoiding wasteful run-offs. Lawns could be watered less frequently, and automobiles and dogs washed monthly instead of weekly.

If the water shortage remains acute over several seasons, long-term changes can be made. For example, utilities may have to invest in more efficient drainage systems to reduce leakages in street mains. In cities where water meters are not universally used, the utility companies may need to install more of them. Hotels will be encouraged to install water-saving shower heads. Industries may have to adopt new water-using equipment, especially in heavy industries that depend on high water use. 'Some steel mills use 65 000 gallons of water per ton produced, but the Kaiser steel mill (in the Los Angeles area) has reduced it to 1600 gallons' (Alchian and Allen, 1972: 66).

In residential areas, higher water prices may encourage smaller gardens and lawns. Rock gardens, paved yard areas and brick patios may become more prevalent. It has been estimated that a doubling of water prices could reduce domestic household water consumption by 30–50 per cent within a year, depending on the region (Redd, 1992; Wichelns and Cone, 1992).

In sum, the overall demand for water, an essential ingredient of life, can be surprisingly elastic.

Given the issues of water shortages, pollution and cost efficiency, many local and state governments around the world are also entertaining the possibility of privatization of the water supply. The object is to reduce the cost of supplying water to residential and industrial users. A recent study by the Reason Foundation demonstrates that the average cost per connection is $547 for government-owned water companies compared to $426 for privately owned water companies. Public water utilities employ more workers per 1000 connections and pay higher salaries than their private counterparts (Neal, 1996). Europe, in particular, has moved toward privatization recently. Britain and France have turned ownership or management of water delivery and treatment over to private companies, such as Thames Water PLC and Lyonnaise des Eaux. Given local governments' current budget limitations, interest in privatization is also growing in the United States (Ferguson, 1996).

M.S.

REFERENCES

Alchian, Armen A. and William R. Allen (1972), *University Economics*, 3rd edn, Belmont, California: Wadsworth Publishing.
Ferguson, Tim W. (1996), 'Socialized Water', *Forbes*, 11 March, pp. 68–70.
Neal, Kathy (1996), *Restructuring America's Water Industry*, Report 200, Los Angeles: Reason Foundation.
Redd, Adrienne (1992), 'Pricing Water by the Gallon', *American City and County*, **107** (2), February, 48–53.
Wichelns, Dennis and David Cone (1992) 'Tiered Pricing Motivates Californians to Conserve Water', *Journal of Soil and Water Conservation*, **47** (2), March, 139–44.

4. The case of the fourth egg

The law of declining marginal utility states that each additional good provides less benefit to the user. But suppose it takes four eggs to bake a cake. In that case, the marginal utility of the first, second and third egg has much less value than the fourth egg, because with the fourth egg, you can now make a cake. The fourth egg has greater utility than the first three because without it a cake cannot be produced properly. How can you square this situation with the law of declining marginal utility?

In this case (made famous by Murray Rothbard) the cake does not violate the law of a downward-sloping demand curve because the two products, although similar in words, are not the same in the eyes of the customer. As stated, the case neglects the fact that a 'good' is not necessarily the physical material, but the product that consumers regard as equally serviceable and interchangeable.

In the cake example above, the four-egg cake is *not* equally serviceable and interchangeable with the one-, two- or three-egg cake. The three- and four-egg cakes are not units of the same supply, and, therefore, the law of diminishing marginal utility does not apply in this case. The only way to apply the law of marginal utility in this situation is to treat each set of four eggs as a homogeneous unit.

In a similar vein, critics of utility theory have sometimes argued that the law of diminishing wants does not always work, based on principles of psychology. For example, an individual may enjoy a second scoop of ice cream more than the first, and therefore marginal utility may increase at first before declining. But this example misconceives the meaning of the law of diminishing marginal utility. The situation of psychological or physiological wants is not the issue, only the idea that the most urgent wants will always be chosen first as a matter of the logic of human action toward a given end. In the example cited, the end changed and so the second scoop of ice cream (sequentially) must have become the first scoop for a new end. Thus the ice cream example does not violate this law (Rothbard, 1970: 63–4).

M.S.

REFERENCE

Rothbard, Murray N. (1970 [1962]) *Man, Economy and State*, Los Angeles: Nash Publishing.

5. Profiting from pants

Terry's Threads prices the popular Panther pants at $20 a pair and sells 1000 pairs. Clara's Clothier in the same area sets the price at $30 a pair and sells 600 pairs. Who is the more perceptive purveyor of Panther pants?

Many people will calculate the revenue received from the sale of Panther pants without considering the differing costs of the two producers. That is, they will consider demand but not supply.

To answer this problem correctly requires us to consider the elements of supply along with demand for Panther pants. These include the wholesale cost of each pair of pants to the retailer, the marginal selling cost of each pair of pants, the amount bought for sale by the retailer, and the salvage value of the pants. We compare this to the revenue received from the sale in each case. There are many possibilities, but we will confine our discussion to three cases.

CASE A: IDENTICAL WHOLESALE PLUS SELLING COSTS OF PANTHER PANTS

If each seller sells all the pants ordered and both paid the same cost per pair to the wholesaler and had the same per pair selling costs, then Clara's Clothier probably, but not certainly, selected a price that will make more profit than Terry's Threads. Even though Clara's total revenue was $2000 less than that of Terry's ($20 × 1000 – $30 × 600), Clara's total cost was most likely more than $2000 less because of the cost of buying and selling many fewer pairs. This is true as long as the combined wholesale plus selling cost of the Panther pants was more than $5 per pair. For example, at $6 per pair wholesale plus selling cost, Terry's makes a profit of $14 000 ($14 × 1000) while Clara's makes a profit of $14 400 ($24 × 600) with the profit margin becoming greater the higher the wholesale plus selling cost is above $5 per pair. Below costs of $5 a pair, Terry's will make a larger profit.

CASE B: NOT ALL PANTHER PANTS SOLD

If each seller did not sell all the pants ordered, then the identity of the profit-maximizing seller also depends on the amount bought for sale and the salvage value of the pants for Clara's. For example, suppose that both stores bought 1000 pairs of pants for $4 each plus $2 selling costs. Assume that the salvage value (i.e. the price that the remainder can be sold for) is $5. As in Case A the profit for Terry's is $14 000. However, the profit for Clara's is now also $14 000, $400 less than in Case A because 400 pairs @ $6 cost were not sold initially but were sold ultimately @ $5/pair, leading to a loss of $400. Would Clara's have been better off not to sell these pants at a loss? Most likely not. The initial wholesale cost does not matter since it is sunk and cannot be regained in any case. Sunk costs are always irrelevant to profit maximizing decisions. Clara's may make less than Terry's by selling Panther pants for salvage value, but Clara's will most likely do better than she would have done by not selling them for salvage value. The only relevant cost at this point is the selling cost. As long as the salvage value is greater than the selling cost, Clara's will do better by selling the remaining Panther pants.

CASE C1: DIFFERENT SELLING COSTS AND NO EXCESS INVENTORY

Now suppose that the previous conditions are all the same as in Case A except that Clara's Clothier and Terry's Threads have different selling costs. Clara's pays higher wages and has more salespeople than Terry's. Terry's also does not offer coffee to customers as does Clara's. Consequently, Clara's selling costs per sale are $5 instead of Terry's $2. Who will make more profit? Clearly, Terry's will still make a $14 000 profit. Clara's makes a profit of only $12 600 ($21 × 600).

CASE C2: DIFFERENT SELLING COSTS AND EXCESS INVENTORY

Now suppose that the previous conditions are all the same as in Case B except that Clara's Clothier and Terry's Threads have different selling costs. Clara's pays higher wages and has more salespeople than Terry's. Terry's also does not offer coffee to customers, as does Clara's. Consequently, Clara's selling costs per sale are $5 instead of Terry's $2. Which store will make more profit? Clearly, Terry's will still make a $14 000 profit. However, the profit for Clara's is now $12 800, $1600 less than in Case A because 400 pairs @ $9 cost were not sold initially but were sold ultimately @ $5/pair, leading to a loss of $1600. Notice that in this case since the per pair salvage value is equal to the selling cost, Clara's is indifferent to selling Panther pants for salvage since the profit will be the same in either case. At a selling cost above $5/pair, the excess clothes bought will not be sold by Clara's – at least by salespeople – since there is no profit in doing so.

K.C.T.

6. The price of quality

Bogg Downe wants to buy a car and budgetary concerns have prompted him to consider the used car market. Not knowing much about the used car market Bogg sought the advice of several friends. Wanda Most told him to look at the price as an indicator of quality because 'you always get what you pay for'. Penny Pincher told him to 'shop for the least expensive car you desire'. Wylie Deals told him, 'when you buy a used car you buy somebody's problem'. Whose advice should Bogg take?

Each piece of advice is somewhat conflicting so it would seem that they cannot all be right. Which one is most useful to Bogg depends on the exact nature of his demand for used cars, the resources he wants to devote to shopping, and the nature of the market in which he is shopping.

'You always get what you pay for.' Wanda Most conveys a popular economic nostrum that is true only under the strongest assumptions about the efficiency characteristics of the market and the simplest assumptions about the perception of quality. Wanda assumes that price is an unerring and proportionate indicator of quality, and she also implies that anyone in the market has the same perception of what quality means.

The price of a used car reflects the interaction of market supply and demand that mutually determine the price and quantity for that car. Market supply and demand each comprise the summation of all potential buyers for (demand) and sellers of (supply) used cars. In turn each individual supply and demand schedule for used cars is shaped by several elements. For a buyer this consists of the prices of related goods, current income, the expectations about future prices of this and related goods, future expected income to be had, and the pure taste for the good. For a seller of used cars this consists of the resource costs of selling the car and the selling techniques available. Together these elements define the level and sensitivity of the market quantity of a used car to its price.

The quality of an item is its perceived utility to a purchaser and has two different dimensions. Its physical or service characteristics are objective and measurable, while its image characteristics are subjective and difficult to measure. Price will be a good indicator of the quality of a used car if the used car market is highly competitive. Competitive markets assume, among other things, that all buyers and sellers have the same information about the nature of the used cars and their prices. Equilibrium means that surpluses and shortages have been eliminated so that prices are stable. If these conditions hold, the differential prices of used cars among sellers in a market area closely reflect the qualitative differences among cars as perceived by the aggregate of consumers of used cars.

Suppose that a perfectly competitive market in equilibrium reveals that a two-year-old used Cheetah automobile sells for $30 000 while a similarly equipped two-year-old Gargoyle sells for only $15 000. In an important sense we can say that the Cheetah has twice the quality of the Gargoyle because in perfectly competitive markets in equilibrium all the information about the used cars on both the demand side and supply side has been accounted for and processed by the market.

However, this does not necessarily help Bogg Downe, for he does not care that price reflects some differential quality as revealed by the amalgamation of consumers' desires and suppliers' costs in the used car market. To use Wanda's advice he needs to be able to use price differentials to *determine* quality, a different matter altogether. For example, it may be that consumers on the average may be willing to pay substantially more for the Cheetah than the Gargoyle automobile because of the former's image of sleekness and speed even though the service characteristics of the two automobiles are virtually identical. If Bogg Downe desires these image characteristics he will gladly pay the $30 000 needed for the Cheetah, but if these image characteristics do not mean much to him relative to the service characteristics he will be happier buying the $15 000 Gargoyle. In order for price to be an unerring indicator of quality for everyone, thus validating the nostrum, everyone's tastes in used cars must be the same. Obviously this is unlikely to be the case. Moreover, the assumption that used car markets are competitive and that they are perpetually in equilibrium is more useful to economists constructing models than to consumers trying to buy cars. In particular the assumption that everyone in the market has equal information about used cars is unrealistic. Let's look at the second bit of advice given to Bogg.

'Shop for the least expensive car you desire.' Penny Pincher recommends the virtues of thrifty shopping and the belief that a bargain is always available if you make the effort to find it. This advice turns out to be true under a variety of conditions, including markets that are neither perfectly competitive nor in equilibrium.

In the last example we took it for granted that all the prices prevailing in the used car market reflect the differential quality of the used cars as the aggregate of buyers perceive that quality. However, if the used car market is not competitive or prices are not in equilibrium then at any point in time different sellers of the same type of used car may be offering it for very different prices. Prices *per se* then convey much less information to Bogg and other consumers. Those consumers who research the characteristics and reliability of various used cars, and who assess the mechanical condition of a particular used car, stand to gain by paying less for a given level of satisfaction than those who do not engage in these activities. What Bogg needs to do here is to estimate the cost to him of the time and effort needed to discover a better used car at a lower price against the differential price and quality gains he hopes to make. That is, he will compare the additional benefits of shopping with the additional costs of shopping. Note here that we have broadened the typical definition of cost. To validate the advice given by Penny Pincher we need to understand that the 'expense' of a car includes the cost of shopping for price and quality.

We do have evidence that some markets are not competitive or not in equilibrium. The continued success of consumer magazines such as *Consumer Reports* and *Consumers Digest* demonstrate that the nostrum 'you always get what you pay for' is unlikely to be true for many people. This would certainly apply to different brands of used cars, whose relative physical quality assessment is featured prominently in these magazines and in others as well. Let's look now at the third observation offered to Bogg.

'When you buy a used car you buy somebody's problem.' Wylie Deals offers an often heard nostrum specifically about the used car market. Is there anything different about this market compared to other markets that would prompt such advice? It turns out that there may be, and the rationale for this comes from George Akerlof (1970) who discusses the 'market for lemons' and uses used cars as his primary example.

The used car market is characterized by asymmetric information. This is a structural problem with some markets in that they do not provide buyers and sellers with equal access to information, and this problem is not solved by competition and equilibrium outcomes. Its effect is to make Bogg legitimately wary and unwilling to pay as high a price as he would were the market not characterized by asymmetric information.

One of the virtues of competition in a market system is that buyers and sellers have a strong incentive to provide useful and correct information in order to maximize their satisfaction. Misinformation increases the costs of transactions and so makes purchases more costly. But in some markets this incentive is weak. An automobile is long-lived and consumes a substantial portion of most people's budgets. The demand for an automobile is also rather inelastic since there are few attractive substitutes as transportation alternatives. Consequently, consumers often do not willingly part with their autos because they will have to buy another for transportation, and they are expensive. That is, they often tend to hold on to them unless they become unreliable transportation.

Because of the technical complexity of the automobile, it may be difficult for the buyer (individuals or dealers) to determine if a specific car has problems and what they are. Both sellers and buyers know this, and so there is a strong tendency for potential sellers not to sell their well-conditioned used cars. Buyers will pay less for a car in general to compensate them for their greater uncertainty as compared with the sellers' about the condition of any used car. Because buyers know that a substantial portion of used cars are 'lemons', and they realize that they do not have the detailed knowledge to determine which ones are the lemons, they will pay less for any of them than were there no or few lemons. A set of behaviours is dynamically generated that tends to 'lemonize' the used car market.

Many buyers of used cars verify their suspicions of poor used cars by their buying experience, and they convey this knowledge to other potential buyers who drop out of the market or demand a premium (i.e. low buying price) to buy. Sellers of good used cars are increasingly less likely to sell them because they cannot get a fair price for their car based on the condition they know it is in but cannot credibly convey to others. Thus there is adverse selection of sellers as the used cars offered for sale tend increasingly to be lemons. Prices fall but not as rapidly as quality falls and thus the value (price/quality) of used cars falls in the market (Stiglitz, 1993, 499–500). In effect a new nostrum applies to this market: 'You get less than you pay for.' If buyers and sellers are completely rational, in the end the used car market could disappear altogether.

Obviously this scenario has not happened. It has not happened because institutions have developed to convey the quality of used cars better or to reduce the uncertainty in buying a used car. Garages and mechanics offer to inspect used cars for defects as a standard service. Some states have passed 'lemon' laws that require sellers (usually dealers) to undertake certain inspections of used cars and to guarantee a certain level of repair should specific physical problems occur with the used car within some period after purchase. At the same time, car manufactures provide multiple warranties on new cars that continue when the car is resold. Used car dealers often provide a limited 30-day, 50/50 warranty for those cars not under the original warranty. Most importantly, private insurers will often insure a car for seven or eight years, for a substantial price, from the time it is new with warranties that are as complete if not more complete than the original manufacturers' warranties.

There are now more state 'lemon' laws, manufacturers' warranties are more complete and longer lived, and private warranties are much more prevalent today in the United States than in 1970 when George Akerlof wrote his well-known article. Using Akerlof's reasoning we can note that these institutional developments have reduced the uncertainty that buyers face in the used car market. The existence of 'lemon' laws and better warranties creates a climate of more trust even if these measures are not used by a particular buyer. Both buyers and sellers of used cars know this. Consequently, sellers are bringing better cars to the used car market, and more buyers are participating in it. In fact the used car market is thriving, so much so that in 1995, new/used car dealers sold a greater dollar value of used cars than new cars in the USA. Does this eliminate the 'lemon' problem? Not completely. As Akerlof noted, even with a warranty, a car buyer still has to incur cost in the time and effort of taking care of the repairs, and this cost cannot be eliminated. With respect to Wylie Deals's nostrum, we can say that there is some truth in it, but it has become less true as institutional changes have allowed the market to deal more effectively with asymmetric information.

K.C.T.

REFERENCES

Akerlof, George (1970), 'The Market for Lemons: Quality Uncertainty and the Market Mechanism', *Quarterly Journal of Economics*, **84**, 488–500.
Stiglitz, Joseph E. (1993), *Economics*, New York: W.W. Norton.

7. The rationality and risk puzzle

Ernest Workman is a financially conservative worker earning $35 000 annually. He has his savings of $10 000 in certificates of deposit at a local bank, and his monthly investment of $200 is divided between well-established bond and blue-chip stock funds. Yet, once or twice a week Ernest spends $10 playing the lottery and makes a once-a-year trip to Biloxi with $1000 to gamble, a trip from which he almost always comes home with little or no cash. Does Ernest, like many others, combine conservative with risky behaviour because he lacks discipline or the education to do otherwise? Or is he simply irrational?

There are several kinds of justification that one could give and have in fact been given for this not uncommon behaviour. Some are more plausible and intellectually appealing than others. But a really attractive answer remains elusive.

One rationalization is that people are simply irrational much of the time, and Ernest's gambling illustrates this. The problem with this solution is that it does not help us understand Ernest's and others' behaviour. Irrationality has no gradations. It cannot be measured even in principle because it serves as a catchall category for behaviours we do not understand, and as such it does not illuminate.

Another possibility is that Ernest may lack the financial discipline to see the apparent inconsistencies in his behaviour. He has the financial discipline to save and invest regularly. But is this enough financial discipline? Would we say he has adequate financial discipline had he only $1000 in savings and put away $50 per month into the same investments? Why does this discipline waver twice a week and disappear once a year? If Ernest does not go to Biloxi next year to gamble, has he then acquired enough financial discipline? This kind of explanation does not provide an appealing understanding of Ernest's behaviour because it gives inadequate guidance as to what constitutes financial discipline for Ernest, not to mention other people. Attributing the problem to education does not help either. We cannot determine the appropriateness of education for financial discipline if we cannot identify what it is. As an amorphous concept, financial discipline cannot be measured, and so the financial discipline associated with different behaviours cannot be assessed.

Another explanation is that Ernest, like many people, is financially conservative and risk-averse when dealing with long-term accumulation of savings or investment. The acts of saving and investing have no utility in and of themselves but are merely vehicles to achieve financial goals. Gambling, on the other hand, is fun, at least for Ernest and others with similar tastes. To be sure, gambling is seen as a vehicle to achieve financial goals, but the act of gambling itself is usually a source of pleasure for those who regularly do it. For Ernest it is the act of gambling and the contemplation of gain while so engaged that motivates him to engage in it, in addition to potential financial gains. Ernest is willing to 'pay' for this pleasure with his gambling losses. Financial economic theory has difficulty dealing with this kind of explanation because it assumes that financial actions taken are motivated both by the utility of the action and the utility of the expected results. This explanation does not provide a way to discriminate between those economic activities, like gambling, that are engaged in for their intrinsic value and those that are instrumental and are not. For example, Ernest could take on the same level of risk/reward tradeoff by buying junk bonds, penny stocks, or commodity options. Why does he prefer to play blackjack instead? Without a theory of means and ends this kind of explanation is *ad hoc* and therefore less appealing.

Perhaps Ernest exhibits *loss aversion*. This means that gains are worth less than equivalent losses, a phenomenon observed in numerous contexts, and held by some cognitive psychologists (Kahneman and Tversky, 1984) to be an innate characteristic of humans. The idea is that people place more subjective value on the financial value of something they already own than on something not yet owned or still to be acquired. Gambling winnings have the latter characteristic, while saving and investing are done to preserve and extend the already gained financial value. Loss aversion explains the adage, 'a bird in the hand is worth two in the bush', and interestingly, this two units of value lost $(-2x)$ for one unit of value gained (x) seems to be an approximate description of reality (Tversky and Kahneman, 1991) as illustrated by Figure 7.1. A loss-aversion explanation can be combined with the concept of gambling as a positively valued activity to yield more gambling gains and more gambling losses than either explanation provides by itself. The loss-aversion explanation is troublesome for mainstream economics because it implies that the opportunity cost concept should be treated asymmetrically, giving a significantly smaller value for gains than for losses. Why should a \$1 gain be equivalent to a \$2 loss?

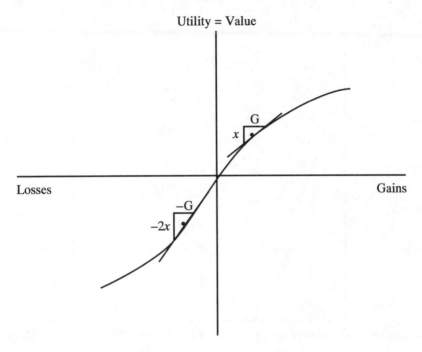

Figure 7.1   Marginal utility of gains and losses

Constraining the opportunity cost concept with an unexplained empirical regularity does not appeal to conceptually oriented mainstream economic thinking.

   A final explanation starts out by assuming that people are economically rational. Economically rational individuals have consistent preferences directed towards well-defined goals. Consistent preferences mean that an individual has underlying preferences that are fully specified and understood by the individual, preferences that are revealed by actual choices made, and which do not change. Decisions are motivated by the marginal opportunity costs of the options to the individual independently of the options themselves or the context in which the options are presented or offered. Unchanging preferences or 'tastes' include risk characteristics. Risk-taking behaviour is neither rational nor irrational *per se*, but switching between risk-taking and risk-avoiding behaviour without reason is irrational behaviour. For Ernest Workman this means that whatever the mix of risk-avoiding and risk-taking behaviour he possesses, it remains constant over time. If Ernest is risk-taking in one situation, he will be equally risk-taking in other similar circumstances. The key phrase here is, of course, 'similar circumstances'.

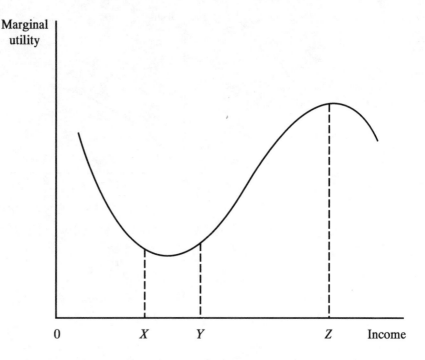

Figure 7.2   Marginal utility of income changes

Friedman and Savage (1948) handled this by postulating that individuals have a utility function such that they tend to be risk-averse when dealing with larger amounts of money than they normally deal with and are more risk-taking when dealing with smaller amounts of money than normal, as determined by their income circumstances. For Ernest's marginal utility (MU) function, shown in Figure 7.2, suppose that his income of $35 000 is in the *X–Y* range. In this range a small loss of income leads to a small loss of utility. Thus we could explain why Ernest plays the lottery. His potential gain is great because the high potential payoff moves him substantially into the increasing marginal utility range, *Y–Z*. Despite the apparent risky nature of playing the lottery, the value of the loss (dollars lost × MU income lost) is less than the expected value of the gain (dollars gained × probability of gain × MU income gain), and so it is rational for Ernest to play the lottery. A $1000 loss will likely push Ernest to the increasing marginal utility range of income just to the left of the midpoint of the *X–Y* range. Combined with the size of the dollar loss it would be improbable that the large value of the loss could be compensated for by the expected value of the gain if he is risk-averse since $1000 annually represents a sizeable part of his long-term income. While this explains his lottery behaviour, it does not explain his annual gambling trip to Biloxi very well. The more money Ernest loses from the $35 000, the higher the marginal utility of the loss per dollar, as shown in Figure 7.2.

We can make more sense of Ernest's behaviour if the gambling trip has intrinsic value and not just the instrumental value of increasing his wealth. Evidently, no single explanation completely explains Ernest Workman's behaviour. Intrinsic value attached to gambling activities, loss aversion and a Friedman–Savage utility function can be combined into a story to explain Ernest's behaviour, but this is not entirely satisfactory since the theories from which each derives are not consistent with each other. A better explanation of this puzzle remains elusive.

K.C.T.

REFERENCES

Friedman, M. and L.J. Savage (1948), 'The Utility Analysis of Choices Involving Risk', *The Journal of Political Economy*, **56**, 279–304.

Kahneman, Daniel and Amos Tversky (1984), 'Choices, Values, and Frames', *American Psychologist*, **39**, 341–50.

Tversky, Amos and Daniel Kahneman (1991), 'Loss Aversion and Riskless Choice: A Reference Dependent Model', *Quarterly Journal of Economics*, **106** (4), 1039–60.

8. Gold's backward supply curve

In the 1970s, gold prices skyrocketed while mining companies reduced their gold output. The production of gold actually declined during the 1970s, then increased substantially in the 1980s – when the price of gold fell. What was the rationale for this behaviour?

Since 1970, when the world left a gold exchange standard and the price of gold fluctuated freely, there has been a rather perverse relationship between the price of gold and the output of gold. Figure 8.1 demonstrates the inverse relationship.

The law of supply and demand states that an increasing price of good *X* will encourage producers to produce more, not less, of good *X*. But in the case of gold, the relationship between price and output suggests

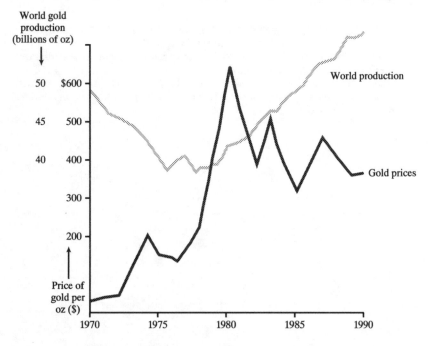

Figure 8.1   World gold production and the price of gold, 1970–90

a backward-bending supply curve. The higher the price, the less is produced, and vice versa.

Some mining experts confirm this perverse relationship. The president of Homestake Mining Company, the oldest gold mining company in the USA, said in 1974, when gold output was declining, 'Over the years, I expect gold production will continue to drop – the faster the price of gold rises, the faster the drop. If gold were at $300 an ounce, I think gold production would be something like a half or a third what it is now' (Jastram, 1977: 187).

Mining experts also note that South Africa, the world's largest gold producer, has a policy of mining ore of the lowest profitable grade at the prevailing gold price. Thus, if the price of gold rises and the rise is seen as a permanent increase in the demand for gold, South African mining companies will shift resources from higher-ore bodies to lower-ore bodies. They will dig deeper into shafts that are most costly and less productive. The initial response, then, to higher gold prices is lower current production of gold.

However, in the long run, there will be strong incentives to increase gold production. In North America and other areas of the world, higher gold prices also mean that mining companies will increase substantially their exploratory and developmental operations. Mines that were previously marginal losers may now be marginally profitable. Again, current production drops as mining companies shift operations, equipment and resources to find and develop new mines.

The solution to this apparent enigma now becomes clear. The backward-bending supply curve for gold represents gold's *short-term* supply curve. Its long-term supply curve is positively sloped, the normal case; see Figure 8.2. Thus a rise in the expected future price of gold shifts resources from current production to future production. The effect is to exchange a *short-term* reduction in gold output for a *long-run* increase in gold production. The rise in the price of gold encourages mining companies to explore and develop new mines, mines that would produce more gold in the future. Indeed, that is what happened. In the 1970s, as the price of gold skyrocketed from $35 an ounce to over $800, new mines were being opened everywhere, and they finally started producing gold in the 1980s. By the time gold's price started dropping in the 1980s this new gold came on stream, and has continued throughout the 1980s and 1990s.

M.S.

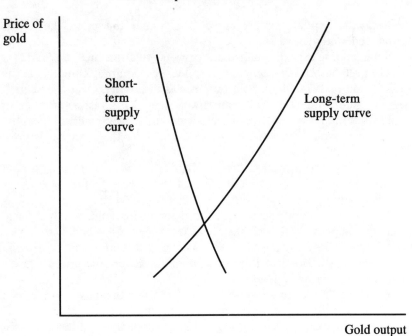

Figure 8.2   Short-term and long-term supply curve for gold

REFERENCE

Jastram, Roy W. (1977), *The Golden Constant*, New York: John Wiley.

9. The positive sloping demand curve?

The law of demand states that if you raise the price of a product, people buy less of it. Publisher Image Creator prints up a thousand copies of an investment report, which they sell for $10 each. Only a handful are sold. Mr Creator decides to redesign the essay into a special 'executive' report and raise the price to $100 for this 'unique' product. Amazingly, the publisher sells out the entire stock. Has Creator discovered a loophole in the law of a downward-sloping demand curve?

Publisher Image Creator may know his marketing, but he needs a refresher course in economics. To understand what has really taken place, let's look at the basics of the demand schedule. Figure 9.1 shows

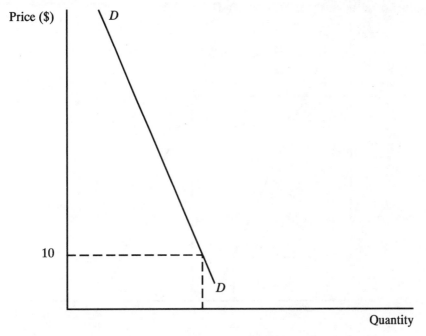

Figure 9.1   Demand schedule for investment report

the demand schedule for commodity *X*, in this case an investment report published by Image Creator. The figure reflects the law of demand: the quantity demanded declines as the price rises. Most importantly, there are several key assumptions made in creating the downward-sloping demand curve, what economists call *ceteris paribus* conditions or 'other things being equal'. These assumptions include: income does not change, tastes stay constant and the product remains the same.

The third assumption is where the confusion arises. For while the publisher does not change the *physical* properties of the investment report (it is still the same copy), he has changed the *aesthetic* properties of the report by calling it something different – a unique 'executive' report promoted through advertising. Consequently, buyers view the investment report as a different product, far superior to the earlier investment report. Image Creator, the marketing genius, has created a new demand curve, substantially to the right of the earlier report, so that the 'new' investment report would sell more copies at every level of price, as can be seen in Figure 9.2.

However, Creator's imaginative ploy does not deny the law of demand. I would venture to guess that if Mr Creator charged $200 for

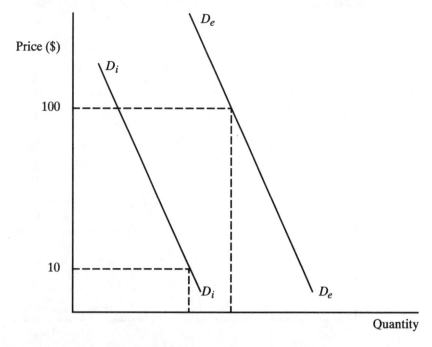

Figure 9.2   New demand curve (D$_e$) *for 'executive' report*

the report, he would get less response than if he charged $100, that is, assuming that the publisher used the same advertising campaign.

Thus we see that the issue is not about countering the law of demand, but taking advantage of all aspects of demand. Advertising has three purposes (Miller, 1994: 568–9):

1. to shift the demand outward (usually by enticing a new group of consumers);
2. to make demand more inelastic (changing consumer perceptions so that the customer perceives fewer substitutes for the product); and
3. to alter demand, so that the good is different and of higher quality (new good).

Mr Creator may be attempting to do all three in his bid to publish an 'executive' investment report.

Not all products are equally susceptible to the marketer's crusades like Image Creator's. Basic generic commodities with little differentiation, low profit margins and in ubiquitous demand by consumers (such as agricultural products) are not likely to respond well to such advertising campaigns. But manufacturers with highly differentiated products, brand loyalty, and high mark-ups (such as perfumes and clothing) are likely to take advantage of this consumerist phenomenon. For example, consumers may not resist a substantial increase in price for a new popular perfume. The demand may be highly inelastic, allowing the producer to capture exceptional profits for a time. Others may not be so lucky. The market is never predictable.

M.S.

REFERENCES

Miller, Roger LeRoy (1994), *Economics Today*, 8th edn, New York: Harper-Collins.

Schmalensee, Richard (1987), 'Advertising', *The New Palgrave: A Dictionary of Economics*, **1**, New York: Macmillan, 34–5.

10.   The leisure paradox

According to the law of supply for labour, the higher the wages the more people are willing to work. Tim Toil earns $10 an hour and works a 40-hour workweek plus an average 10 hours a week in overtime. He gets a raise to $15 an hour, and decides to stop working overtime and spend more time with his family. Does Tim's decision in favour of leisure violate the law of supply for labour?

The leisure paradox suggests the possibility of what economists term a 'backward-bending' supply curve for labour. Normally, the supply curve for labour in the short run is positively sloped: the higher the wages, the more hours wage-earners devote to work. In this analysis, leisure

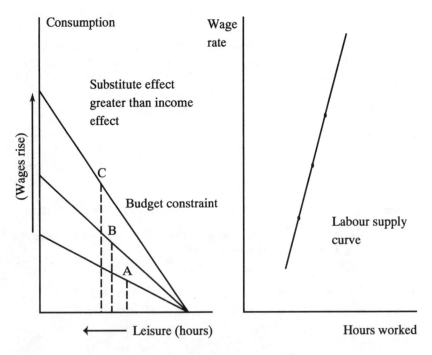

Figure 10.1   Budget constraint and labour supply curve

gives positive utility and work gives negative utility that has to be compensated for by the wage one receives.

We can see this relationship using a budget-constraint figure showing the tradeoff between consumption and leisure time (Stiglitz, 1993: 281–7). In Figure 10.1, wage increases shift the budget constraint upward, since Tim now has more income. In this example, we see how the budget constraint expands as wages rise. The worker works longer hours and therefore cuts back on his leisure hours as the wage increases. The substitution effect is greater than the income effect. The substitution effect refers to Tim giving up leisure to work more, so that, as the figure shows, the labour supply curve is inelastic but positively sloped.

However, as wages increase even further, we encounter a different tradeoff, as shown in Figure 10.2. Here the income effect is greater than the substitution effect. As wages rise, individuals like Tim Toil feel better off, inducing them to work *less* and spend more leisure time. More leisure time, like most goods, is more desirable as income

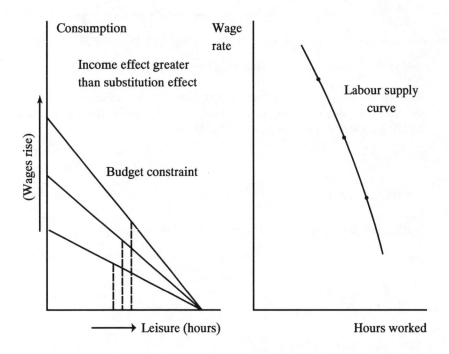

Figure 10.2   Budget constraint and negatively sloping supply curve for labour

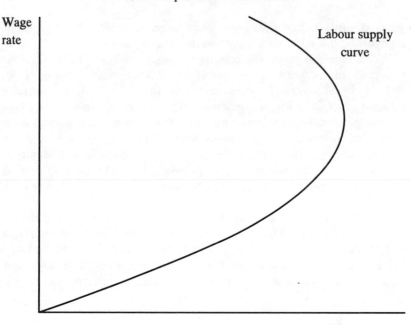

Figure 10.3   Backward-bending supply curve for labour

increases. Doctors, dentists, and other high-income professionals who cut back on their workweek may provide evidence of this backward-bending supply curve, as shown in Figure 10.3.

M.S.

REFERENCE

Stiglitz, Joseph (1993), *Economics*, New York: W.W. Norton.

11. The price discrimination dilemma

Seniors and children pay $3 for the same movie that others pay $6 to see. Virtually the same meal that costs $16 during the evening at Gary's Gourmet costs $9 if one comes between 5:00 and 6:00 p.m. for the 'early bird special'. The practice of charging different prices to different individuals for the same good is called price discrimination. It implies the existence of monopoly power and so is economically inefficient, and it is often illegal. Yet not only is price discrimination pervasive in society, it is an important way in which society covertly and unintendedly redistributes consumption, much of it from the rich to the poor. How?

Price discrimination is the practice of charging more than one price to different individuals for a similar good. Single-price markets may dominate in modern societies, but a little reflection will convince us that multiple-price markets are very important. Price discrimination is practised to increase firm profits. However, its effects on output and welfare relative to single-price firms with monopoly power are likely to be positive. Moreover, much of it tends to make consumption more equal across income classes. Let's see how this happens.

One issue needs to be dealt with to avoid confusion. Cost-based price distinctions are important but not of concern here. Charging a customer more in Rome than in London may reflect nothing more than higher distribution costs for an English manufacturer of cookie cutters. Cost-based price distinctions are legal, socially acceptable, and imply no puzzle or paradox. The kind of price discrimination in which we are interested depends on the fact that different people evaluate the worth of any good or service differently, and therefore price differentials also can occur because of differences in demand, not cost. Price discrimination is demand-motivated, and that creates the puzzling effects alluded to.

Price discrimination exists because in a single-price market what a buyer is willing to pay, his reservation price, usually differs from what he has to pay, the market price. The difference between market price and reservation price creates consumer surplus, and it is a potential source of profits for sellers. In a single-price market there is a great deal of consumer surplus because the price in the market for all units derives from the value attributed by consumers to the last unit consumed, thus making for consumer surplus on the earlier more valuable units consumed. This reflects the fact that the desire for any good or service is subject to the law of diminishing marginal satisfaction, so that the more valuable first units are consumed earlier and less valuable ones are consumed later as the price declines. For example, for Fred Freeby the most important use of water is for drinking to sustain his life, a less important use is to wash his clothes and flush his toilets and an even less important use is to wash his dog and clean his driveway of oil and leaves. But the price Fred pays for water is the low per gallon price of water, reflecting the last uses of the good for the aggregate of all consumers of water. Everyone, like Fred, receives a surplus on all the earlier units (washing clothes, flushing toilets, drinking, etc.) that together we call aggregate consumer surplus. Sellers who successfully construct price discrimination strategies to induce consumers to reveal their reservation prices increase their profits. The existence of price discrimination, because it implies output restrictions associated with monopoly power, means that output is less than it would be and inefficiency exists. However, because price discrimination strategies can, but need not, increase output relative to no price discrimination strategies, their allocative efficiency effects *vis-à-vis* single-price firms with monopoly power are uncertain (Katz and Rosen, 1991: 484–6). Nonetheless, price discrimination has generated significant legislation to prevent it in the USA.

In 1914 the Clayton Act, later amended by the Robinson–Patman Act in 1936, banned price discrimination that was not based on manufacturing, sale, or delivery costs if it lessened or prevented competition in an industry. This legislation also prevented indirect price discrimination through bogus brokerage commissions and the provision of promotional allowances and services to favoured customers. It also allows a seller to lower price to selected customers to meet, but not beat, the competitive pricing practices of others (Blair and Kasserman, 1985: 58–60).

These laws were motivated by business concerns, and in practice they have been used by businesses against the pricing practices of other businesses and not by retail consumers against businesses that provide other consumers with favourable price treatment. Consequently, retail price discrimination is common. Nonetheless, it is not pervasive since several conditions must hold in order for price discrimination among buyers to increase the profits of the seller.

First, a seller must have some monopoly power – some control over the price charged. All but perfectly competitive firms meet this condition. Second, a seller must be able to identify buyers or buyer groups with different intensities of demand for a product. Without identifiably different demand intensities among buyers, price discrimination cannot increase seller profits. Third, the transactions cost of separating the buyers with differential demands must be lower than the differential gain in profit expected from the multiple-price as compared to the one-price strategy. Fourth, a seller must be able to actually separate buyers so that the different prices they charge do not induce reselling by the low-price-paying buyers to the high-price-paying buyers. This fourth condition is commonly met by services since services themselves cannot be resold, and markets are often not developed for service contracts that can be resold, such as automobile warranties. This fourth condition can also be met in the goods market if locational, knowledge, personal resource, or personal taste differences can be identified and are relatively stable among buyers or groups of buyers and these translate into a substantially different willingness to pay.

These four conditions occur in a number of markets in the USA, and price discrimination can be of three types. When each separate buyer pays the price they are willing to pay in a given product market, first-degree price discrimination occurs. In this case all the consumer surplus is absorbed by the seller, and the demand curve becomes the marginal revenue curve for the seller. Complete first-degree price discrimination is virtually impossible to accomplish because it is very costly for the seller to determine what each buyer is willing to pay for each unit. Well-attended auctions probably represent the closest approximation, but even here the winning buyer may have been willing to pay more than the winning bid. Negotiable price markets are also approximations to first-degree price discrimination. These include the negotiable fees of lawn services and private garbage collection, markets which are not perfectly competitive and in which buyers have different intensities or elasticities of demand. In these markets the separation of buyers is made possible because systematic communication among buyers about price/quality characteristics is made difficult by the absence of tradable contracts for such services (such as automobile warranties) or laws prohibiting first-degree price discrimination (such as life and medical insurance regulations).

Second-degree price discrimination occurs when firms charge different prices in a given market depending on the quantity consumed. Since consumers have a downward-sloping demand curve, they will pay less for larger than for smaller quantities. Charging less per unit the more one buys, called quantity discounts, is a typical way a firm can gain some of the consumer surplus that would be forgone by a one-price strategy. Here it is the different level of demand by buyers that allows sellers to gain more profit through consumer surplus with a multiple-pricing strategy. There is a complication. Sellers may also have an incentive to give quantity discounts if the marginal cost of producing extra output is lower. Typically this is not the case as marginal costs tend to be constant or increase as output increases, but it does create some confusion about motivation when businesses give quantity discounts. Second-degree price discrimination has been of concern to businesses because large retail firms with market power over resource suppliers may negotiate for quantity discounts to give themselves a cost advantage over smaller rivals who cannot profitably absorb so much supply. Consequently, quantity discounts can lead to less industry competitiveness, and cases have been brought under the Robinson–Patman Act to address this issue (Blair and Kasserman, 1985: 263–8).

Third-degree price discrimination occurs when sellers alter or position products in submarkets to attract buyer groups with different elasticities of demand. In general to maximize profits a seller will produce an additional unit of product as long as (declining) marginal revenue (MR) is greater than (rising) marginal cost (MC). They stop producing where $MR = MC$, the profit-maximizing output level, and the price charged is given by demand at that output. If two buyer groups, 1 and 2, have substantially different elasticities of demand and can be identified and separated, then a two-price discrimination strategy will be employed. The profit-maximizing condition becomes $MR_1 = MR_2 = MC$. It can be easily shown that $MR = P(1 - 1/E_D)$ where E_D stands for elasticity of demand. Thus for a two-price discriminating firm the profit-maximizing output level is determined by $P_1(1 - 1/E_{D1}) = P_2(1 - 1/E_{D2}) = MC$. From this equality we can see that P increases as E_D declines, so that the price will be higher as E_D is lower or more inelastic.

We can see that an important key to a profitable price discrimination strategy for a seller is to identify groups or submarkets with different demands for a product and charge the higher price to the group or submarket with the more inelastic demand. Car rentals for a single day are more expensive than the daily rate for a weekend or weekly rental because car rental companies assume that the single-day market has proportionally more business travellers and those with more intense or inelastic demand than the weekend and weekly car rental market. The same buyer groups are targeted with higher weekday versus lower Saturday stay-over rates on airline flights. In clothing stores the latest styles are brought in at a higher price to attract a group of buyers whose more inelastic demand reflects their desire to be trend setters. Those who wait will pay less for the same clothes later on when the sales occur. Of course, legitimate overstocking does occur, but most sales are well planned in advance to reap the greater profits that come with this price discrimination strategy. Likewise, couponing and discount deals for restaurants, motels and other services is another important way that businesses can price-discriminate and improve profits. Those individuals whose time is more valuable (to them), and/or for whom these discounting practices are unappealing, will pay the shelf price even though it is higher than it would be in a one-price system.

For some types of third-degree price discrimination, the legality and social acceptability of the buyer group being targeted become important. Differentiating among buyers on the basis of sex, age, or race or a closely related variable is easily done, but in many contexts it is both illegal and socially unacceptable. Banks cannot now, but once did, discriminate among potential borrowers on the basis of race (or location of residence, a proxy for race); nor can auto dealers systematically charge higher prices to women than men. However, our society has deemed it socially acceptable and legal for businesses to give senior citizens and children discounts for numerous goods and services and for bars to give free or discount drinks on the basis of sex, such as on Ladies' Nights.

The effects of first-, second- and third-degree price discrimination in reducing consumer surplus and lowering the price to the buyers with the more elastic demand can be seen in Figure 11.1, where the consumer surplus absorbed by profit-maximizing sellers using different price discriminating strategies is shaded in each of the four panels.

A great deal of third-degree price discrimination is difficult for the buyer to detect because the differential prices faced may partially reflect differential costs, and so profits are increased further. However, cost differences do not motivate the price discrimination strategy. Differential demand does. A good example of this is 'early bird specials' in restaurants in the USA, designed to capture a more price-sensitive market that prefers to eat earlier. It is true that the earlier dinners are usually smaller and so cheaper to produce than the regularly priced dinners. However, cost reduction does not explain the reason for the 'early bird strategy'. Even if early bird consumers would only accept, at a lower price, the identical quantity (and quality) of meals served later in the evening, the restaurant would continue the 'early bird' strategy as long as the extra revenue from the early bird dinners was greater than the extra cost of serving them. The same can be said about airlines' multiple-price strategy. The higher level of comfort and service in first class is more costly for the airlines, but their much higher profit margins on these seats are due to differential demands of the two groups of fliers, and it is this that motivates a price discrimination

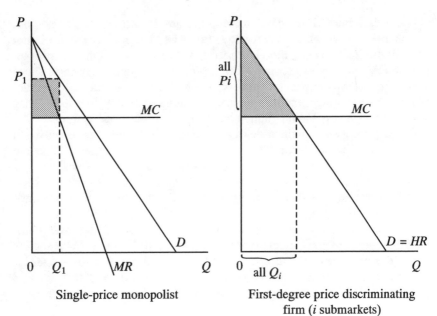

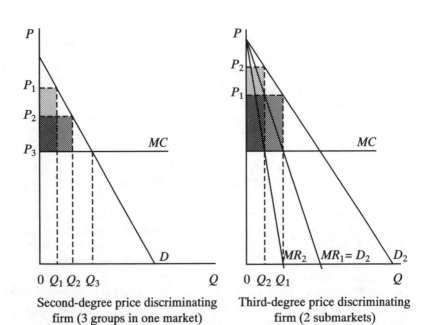

Figure 11.1   Degrees of price discrimination and consumer surplus

strategy. Similar comments can be made about seating in stadiums and arenas. More expensive seating has a much higher profit margin than does regular seating, which is one of the reasons cities are busy building and refurbishing these facilities across the country. We also see price discrimination in markets for goods such as yachts, automobiles and refrigerators where some buyers will pay much more to purchase 'top of the line' or stylistic products for status or for aesthetic purposes even though the functional differences between these and lower-priced models are negligible.

One can, of course, argue that product alteration in different groups of consumers' minds constitutes an adequate basis for calling them separate products and different markets. On this view no third-degree price discrimination ever takes place. However, this linguistic gambit is not helpful since defining products in this way does not affect the efficacy of a multiple-price strategy for the seller. The seller must still look at the four factors earlier noted to determine whether or not a multiple-price strategy will increase profits, whether we choose to call it price discrimination or separate product pricing.

At the most general level a one-price strategy for making profits is simple, but it omits much useful information about the consumers' willingness to pay. The more information about consumers' demand that can be incorporated into a pricing strategy, the greater the profit. This is why there is such a strong and continual motivation for sellers to price-discriminate if they can. The two most important measurable variables, taste being non-measurable, explaining the individual consumer's willingness to pay are his knowledge and income levels.

Price discrimination based on differential knowledge implies higher prices for the less knowledgeable. In such markets consumption is redistributed in favour of the more knowledgeable in relation to single-price markets. It turns out that people's income level is highly correlated with their educational level, a major proxy for knowledge. Thus many knowledge-motivated price discrimination strategies tend to redistribute consumption from the poor to the rich. This happens in markets where the service characteristics of a product are complex or difficult to observe, and advertising and sales create a great deed of noise along with information. Consumer durables like automobiles, yachts and refrigerators, and insurances such as life, disability and health are price-differentiated at least partially on the basis of consumer knowledge.

However, most first- and third-degree price discrimination strategies are associated with the income and wealth levels of consumers. Most goods are normal goods, so that more are preferred by consumers with higher incomes or greater wealth. Negotiable prices such as lawn service and garbage collection are typically lower in lower-income areas. Corporate travellers pay more for car rental and airline seats than leisure travellers of lesser means. Coupon users and discount users have lower incomes than non-users. Senior citizens and children have lower incomes than other age groups. Early bird eaters and sales shoppers also have lower incomes than those who do not. Stylistic and aesthetic concerns may prompt higher-income/education buyers to pay a higher price than do lower-income/education buyers. Any price discrimination strategies that depend on charging a group of buyers a great deal more for a good or service to buy changes that convey status or improve aesthetics, but which cost little, redistribute real consumption to those of lesser means, as compared to a single-price strategy, which implies a higher price for low-income buyers. Price discrimination does lower aggregate consumer surplus and is allocatively less efficient than single-price markets where firms have no monopoly power. However, the alteration of product characteristics and subsequent diversity of product mix implied by most price discrimination strategies increase output and welfare relative to single-price markets consisting of firms with monopoly power. In addition substantial redistribution of consumption takes place with income-driven price discrimination strategies. Since an unambiguous effect of a successful first- or third-degree price discrimination strategy is that the group paying the lower price pays less and buys more than they would under a one-price strategy, there is a real consumption redistribution toward those of lower incomes. Society may regard much of this redistribution as socially and politically desirable even though conventional economic understanding does not address the desirability of such strategies on grounds other than economic efficiency. Measuring the size of this consumption redistribution would be a formidable task, but it is clearly huge and most likely dominates knowledge-based strategies in the aggregate, at least in the USA. If so (for firms with monopoly power), multiple-price strategies not only tend to increase output and economic welfare; they also make consumption distribution more equal than one-price strategies.

K.C.T.

REFERENCES

Blair, Roger D. and David L. Kasserman (1985), *Antitrust Economics*, Homewood, Illinois: Irwin.
Katz, Michael L. and Harvey S. Rosen (1991), *Microeconomics*, Homewood, Illinois: Irwin.

Philips, Louis (1987), 'Price Discrimination', in John Eatwell, Murray Milgate, and Peter Newman (eds), *The New Palgrave: A Dictionary of Economics*, **3**, New York: Stockton Press.
Robinson, Joan (1933), *The Economics of Imperfect Competition*, New York: Macmillan.

12.   A hot vacation spot

The Wall Street Journal (21 July 1995) reported that 'occupancy at Phoenix-area resorts stands well above 70 per cent this summer, up from barely 50 per cent three years ago'. The article offered the view that an important cause of this increase was the rise in hotel room rates. Does this violate the law of demand?

This article provides one of many everyday examples of a simultaneous increase in the price and quantity of a good or service. Economists are naturally suspicious of violations of the law of demand, and in fact have never found one empirically. Consequently, they look to other explanations before considering a violation.

One explanation for the increase in room rates could be that some factor of demand other than price has changed, and this caused the demand for Phoenix hotel rooms to increase. One possible candidate is income change. The article noted that the occupancy rate jumped from 50 per cent in the summer of 1992 to 70 per cent in the summer of 1995. Could it be that aggregate incomes of consumers increased so much between 1992 and 1995 that they were willing to pay a higher price for goods and services generally, including hotel rooms? The data do not support this hypothesis. The increase in income would have to be dramatic to cause such a jump in hotel room consumption rates. GDP per capita increases in 1993, 1994, and mid-1995 (annualized) were 1.1 per cent, 2.5 per cent, and 0.4 per cent respectively (US Department of Commerce). Consequently, income increases cannot be used to explain the event.

The article also points out that Phoenix hoteliers were previously entrapped by their own residents' vision of Arizona as a place of intense and unremitting summer heat. Marketing campaigns for Phoenix hotels began to stress the beneficent effects of the dry Arizona heat and the guaranteed sunshine for the wide variety of outdoor activities available to visitors. A plausible explanation is that many potential consumers were made aware of the advantages of vacationing in the Phoenix area that they were previously unaware of or did not consider important until advertising stimulated their interest. They then became sufficiently interested that the benefits of vacationing there compensated for the costs, and so their taste for such a vacation increased. Consequently, the aggregate demand for Phoenix vacations increased, implying that the demand shifted up and rightwards along the up-sloping supply curve. This implies an increase in the quantity of vacations bought and sold and a higher unit price for them, the results actually observed.

A criticism of the above argument is that, since occupancy only went from 50 per cent to 70 per cent, aggregate supply of rooms had not approached capacity, the point at which we would expect price per room to rise rapidly. That is, the aggregate supply curve for rooms should still be fairly flat so that the shift in demand for rooms should push up the price of rooms little or not at all. This is a plausible argument. What may have happened is that there were a great many potential consumers of Phoenix vacations who had little direct information about the area and for whom it was costly to acquire such information. Phoenix competes with a great many other vacation destinations that may have been better advertised in the past. When consumers are faced with the purchase of a good that has service characteristics which are complex or difficult to discern, they attempt to ascertain, at a reasonable cost, the quality of the product to reduce their uncertainty. One method consumers often use is price, reasoning that if the price of an unknown product is similar to the price of a known product, it must be of similar quality. This is based on the implicit assumption that markets are competitive and tend to produce prices that are similar for similar products. More deeply, the efficient market hypothesis says that equilibrium prices contain all the information available to assess its value. Hoteliers, by raising the prices of rooms to a higher level than would be warranted by conventional demand and supply conditions, made the claims of comfort and good times more credible in the minds of consumers and so increased the demand for Phoenix hotel rooms.

It turns out that traditional supply and demand curves cannot be used to illustrate this because they assume that buyers and sellers are fully informed. For traditional supply and demand situations, price and quantity of a product are mutually determined by the interaction of supply and demand, but each determinant of demand and supply is separable from the other. In this case, because the buyers of these rooms are not fully informed, they use the higher price as a necessary part of the new information that increases their taste for the hotel rooms. Consequently, the increases in taste and price are not separable in demand, and demand and supply analysis does not apply.

One way to get around this problem is to define the newly advertised Phoenix hotel rooms as a different product for which a different set of demand and supply curves apply. In the summer of 1995 this *new product* commanded a higher price than did previous Phoenix hotel rooms. Conceptually, this is a legitimate approach since a new level of information for consumers has been established, and so consumers may see this as a new product. A disappointment with this solution is that it does not help us understand the relationship between information and price, the most interesting aspect of this, and many other similar cases where the physical nature of the good does not change, but the perception of the good changes because of varying degrees of information possessed by consumers.

K.C.T.

REFERENCE

US Department of Commerce, *Survey of Current Business*, various issues.

13. The rare case of a Giffen good?

During the Irish famine of the 1840s, the price of potatoes skyrocketed, but the poor ate less meat and more potatoes! So claimed Sir Robert Giffen, who was allegedly the first to observe this phenomenon. How can you explain the existence of a Giffen good, which appears to contradict the law of demand?

When the price of a commodity rises, people demand less of it. So states the law of demand. The rare case of an upward-sloping demand curve is known as a Giffen good, named after Sir Robert Giffen (1837–1910), a British statistician who allegedly claimed that the consumption of potatoes by the poor rose when their price increased during the Irish potato famine (1845–48).

Although we have no written findings by Giffen, British economist Alfred Marshall referred to Giffen's claim, using bread as an example:

> As Mr Giffen has pointed out, a rise in the price of bread makes so large a drain on the resources of the poorer labouring families and raises so much the marginal utility of money to them, that they are forced to curtail their consumption of meat and the more expensive farinaceous foods: and, bread being still the cheapest food which they can get and will take, they consume more, and not less of it. (Marshall, 1895: 208)

The theoretical justification for a Giffen good is as follows. Since potatoes (or bread) represent such a large proportion of the poor people's diet, if the price of potatoes goes up, the people can no longer afford to buy other foods, such as meat and vegetables, and therefore buy more potatoes instead.

Normally, when the price of a food item goes up, people buy less of it because they can buy a substitute. If the price of butter rises, they may switch to margarine. If the price of beef rises, they may buy more chicken. Economists refer to this as the 'substitution effect'.

But there is also a separate 'income effect' from a price change. As the price of a good rises, real income or purchasing power is reduced. So, as the price of butter rises, real income available to purchase all goods falls and less butter is purchased.

There are, however, some goods that we want to purchase more of when real income falls. These are called 'inferior' goods simply because as income rises we want less of them. Margarine and chicken are examples. When their price falls, we substitute them for butter and beef, respectively. At the same time, however, we see our real income rising and, on this ascent, we purchase less of them because they are inferior goods. Which effect dominates? Invariably the substitution effect is more powerful than the income effect, and so we get the expected result that when prices of chicken or margarine fall, we buy more of them.

Giffen believed he had discovered an exception with potatoes. Because potatoes captured such a large proportion of the poor's budget, when the price of potatoes rose, the income effect of this inferior good dominated the substitution effect and the poor consumed more potatoes after the rise in price.

Economists use indifference curve analysis to demonstrate the possibility, however rare, of a Giffen good. Figure 13.1 demonstrates the case of a normal good, where the substitution effect is far greater than

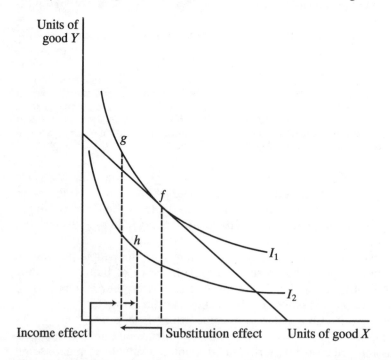

Figure 13.1 Normal case: substitution effect is greater than the income effect

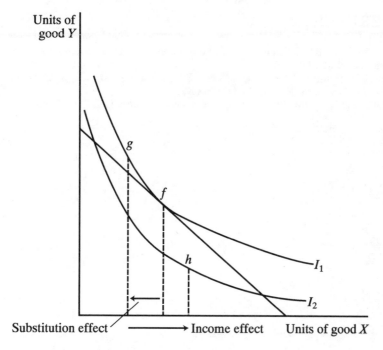

Figure 13.2   Giffen good: income effect exceeds substitution effect

the income effect. Normally, the rise in the price of one food has little effect on a person's income. Hence a rise in the price of potatoes will normally cause people to buy fewer.

But what if potatoes form a large proportion of a person's diet? In that case, the income effect may offset the substitution effect. Since potatoes are an inferior good, a sharp reduction in a person's income may cause him to buy more potatoes, not less. Figure 13.2 shows the case of a Giffen good.

Because isolated price increases do not significantly affect the real income of individual consumers, Giffen goods are likely to be rare (Dougan, 1982). As yet there has been no empirical verification of its existence, even during the Irish potato famine (Dywer and Lindsay, 1984).

M.S.

REFERENCES

Dougan, W. R. (1982), 'Giffen goods and the law of demand', *Journal of Political Economy*, **90** (4), 809–15.
Dwyer, G. P., Jr and C. W. Lindsay (1984), 'Robert Giffen and the Irish Potato', *American Economic Review*, **74** (1), 188–92.
Marshall, Alfred (1895), *Principles of Economics*, 3rd edn, London: Macmillan.

14.   The case of the costly catsup

Why do supermarket items such as peanut butter, tuna fish and catsup often sell for more per ounce in larger sizes as compared to smaller sizes? Is this a violation of the law of downward-sloping demand?

Charging a higher unit price for large sizes than small sizes turns out to be a common phenomenon in supermarkets, despite the popular consumers' assumption that larger items tend to be sold for quantity discounts. These quantity surcharges would seem to be a violation of the law of downward-sloping demand, but evidence to date suggests the phenomenon instead results from the ability of sellers to price-discriminate.

In a one-price market consumer surplus occurs because different consumers have different intensities of preference. The price any buyer pays only reveals the minimum he is willing to pay, not the maximum. Consequently, additional 'consumer surplus' can be turned into a larger profit if the seller can create socially acceptable ways to charge different prices for the same or a similar good to different consumers – that is, to *price-discriminate*. One method used by both manufacturers and grocers has been to produce and accept discount coupons for grocery items. Those whose demand and shopping costs are high, and so are less price-sensitive, do not bother to clip coupons, and others who do clip coupons receive the benefit of lower prices. This coupon-issuing strategy produces more profit than charging any single price because it uses more information about consumer demand. Another strategy offered by manufacturers is to offer a premium upgrade to a popular brand. The use of words such as 'select', 'premium', 'super', 'new', 'extra' or 'ultra' added to a product name along with different packaging can entice some consumers to pay a higher price than that of the regular brand, thereby gaining some of the consumer surplus and greater profits. Another strategy that grocers have been using to gain some price discrimination profit has been to employ quantity surcharges.

In the USA the use of quantity surcharges is well documented in the grocery industry (Agrawal, Grimm and Srinivasan, 1993: 336, 348). Both manufacturer and grocer supply-side and consumer demand-side factors could explain their existence. One possible supply-side influence could be higher unit costs of packaging larger sizes for manufacturers. For example, heavier cartons may be needed for larger sizes or larger sizes may take up proportionally more space in refrigerated trucks. Another supply-side factor could be higher grocery storage costs. This could occur for two reasons. First, the nature of the item stored and the packaging might mean that a size that has double the amount of consumer product takes up more than twice the scarce space on grocery shelves, produce bins, or the freezer. Second, larger sizes may have lower product turnover rates, which implies the greater relative use of storage space over time compared to smaller sizes, an outcome that is reflected in the fact that profit margins tend to be set higher on low-turnover products. Each of these supply factors would justify a higher unit cost, or quantity surcharge, levied by the grocer for a larger size product. On the other hand, lower unit packaging costs of larger sizes could imply just the opposite, quantity discounts (Walden, 1988). This set of supply factors implies that quantity surcharging might be a profitable strategy, but does not imply a conscious price discrimination strategy since the factors are based on measurable accounting cost considerations and not demand considerations.

Possible consumer demand-side influences that would induce a customer to buy a larger size include low consumer storage costs (Gerstner and Hess, 1987), high time search costs (Salop, 1977), high overall demand, low desire to compare prices, and high desire for large packages *per se* (Agrawal, Grimm and Srinivasan, 1993: 342). Each of these demand factors, if relevant and identifiable, would tend to make quantity surcharges a profitable price discrimination technique for the grocer.

A study which attempted to assess a number of these factors was recently completed using 62 different high-volume products in the Buffalo, New York area (Agrawal, Grimm and Srinivasan, 1993) and running two regression equations on grocery shopper survey data. For consumer demand these authors discovered that the propensity to buy a large package was primarily influenced by household demand. Consumer time search costs, storage costs, and desire to compare prices were all significant influences on propensity to buy a large package, and in the right direction, but their quantitative importance was together much less than that of overall demand. For grocers these authors found that the likelihood of a quantity surcharge being levied as measured by the incidence of quantity surcharging – the proportion of a given product's package sizes that are quantity-surcharged – depends primarily and positively on two variables: the percentage of users of a product and the likelihood of a household buying a large package, both of which are demand, not cost, considerations used by the seller.

What is clear from this study is that consumer demand for a product is a primary determinant of whether or not manufacturers and grocers see it as a viable candidate for quantity surcharges, and these are the influences that suggest a price discrimination strategy. Still there is much more to learn about this issue.

Less than 50 per cent of the variation in the propensity to buy a large package was explained by the above variables on the consumer demand side and only slightly more than 25 per cent of the likelihood of levying a quantity surcharge by grocers was explained by the percentage of users of a product and the likelihood of a household buying a large package. Moreover, the influence of high storage costs was not examined and neither was the influence of the turnover rate because the products selected were all high-volume sellers. Consequently, the study was biased towards looking for demand-side influences.

Moreover, an important dimension of price discrimination is missing from this and other studies, which did not look at the size of the quantity surcharge and attempt to estimate what portions of it were due to which factors. Such a study would be a more revealing approach than looking at quantity surcharge incidence across products since different incidence across products could be explained by different marketing strategies of the manufacturers of different products. Such an explanation assumes that quantity surcharges are levied by the manufacturer rather than the grocer, an issue which these studies also do not directly address. In addition, economic theory suggests that if quantity surcharges persist in incidence and size over time, consumers would come to understand this, reducing consumer search costs and shifting many purchases away from larger sizes. Quantity surcharges due to price discrimination would then become less and less prevalent over time. Ultimately, the remaining quantity surcharges would be due to purely supply-side factors of higher production or storage costs and/or low turnover rates. Only if grocers levy random quantity surcharges across products could profits due to price discrimination be maintained since this would keep consumer search costs from declining.

Ignorance and its institutionalization may well play an important role in perpetuating quantity surcharges. One study noted that barely more than half of those surveyed knew the prices of grocery items for which they shopped within 5 per cent (Dickson and Sawyer, 1990). If we combine randomly assigned quantity surcharges, the existence of the institution of 'quantity discounting' which creates a mind set that negates price search under the consumers' assumption that the larger item invariably has the lowest unit price, and grocers positioning themselves as good-value or discount sellers, we have a complex of factors that creates a great deal of 'price-search cost noise'. This noise makes simple price-search *rules of thumb*, formulated to reduce the costly process of price searching for every item, much less successful for the consumer. In such an environment consumer use of rules of thumb such as 'I will buy at Wally's Discount Foods' or 'I will buy Henrietta's extra large pickled cabbage because all her products tend to be cheaper' will make a price discrimination strategy very successful for the seller.

Nonetheless, more information on the degree of quantity surcharging and whether supply-side factors are important is needed to resolve this puzzle.

K.C.T.

REFERENCES

Agrawal, Jagdish, Pamela E. Grimm and Narasimhan Srinivasan (1993), 'Quantity Surcharges on Groceries', *The Journal of Consumer Affairs*, **27** (2), 335–56.
Dickson, Peter R. and Alan G. Sawyer (1990), 'The Price Knowledge and Search of Supermarket Shoppers', *Journal of Marketing*, **54**, 42–53.
Gerstner, Eitan and James D. Hess (1987), 'Why Do Hot Dogs Come in Packs of 10 and Buns in 8s or 12s?' Journal of Business, **60** (4), 491–517.
Salop, Steven (1977), 'The Noisy Monopolist: Imperfect Information, Price Dispersion and Price Discrimination', *Review of Economic Studies*, **44**.
Walden, Michael (1988), 'Why Unit Prices of Supermarket Products Vary', *The Journal of Consumer Affairs*, **22**, 74–84.

15. The mail order question

A mail order publisher tests two prices for the same book, $15 and $25. He mails each ad to 5000 randomly selected names from a list of book buyers. One hundred people order the book for $25, resulting in gross revenues of $2500, while 200 people respond to the $15 offer, with gross revenues of $3000. The mail order publisher decides to advertise all future books for $25. Did he make a mistake?

Clearly the $15 order brought in the most revenue, so if one were to judge solely on the basis of gross revenues, the publisher should charge $15 for the book. He made the wrong choice. However, the most important consideration is not gross revenue, but total profits. The mail order publisher must consider gross revenues minus his costs. Unless we know the cost structure of the business, it is difficult to say which price he should charge.

Suppose that it costs $10 to advertise, print and fulfil each book order. Let's also suppose that the publisher plans to roll out his ad to a mailing list of a million book buyers. Based on his initial test of 5000 names, he will sell approximately 100 000 books at $25 each, or 200 000 books at $15 each. His total profits are given in Table 15.1; Figure 15.1 demonstrates the situation. Thus we see that although the lower price brings in more revenue, the higher price brings in more profit. Therefore, the publisher made the right decision.

Table 15.1   Book profit for an undifferentiated customer base

For $25 book		For $15 book	
Gross revenues	$2.5 million	Gross revenues	$3.0 million
Gross costs	$1.0 million	Gross costs	$2.0 million
Total profit	$1.5 million	Total profit	$1.0 million

But did he? There are two other factors that publishers should not ignore, factors that could alter his decision once again. (Isn't business fun?) One is the possible economies of scale in printing and fulfilling orders for 200 000 books instead of 100 000 books. If by selling 200 000

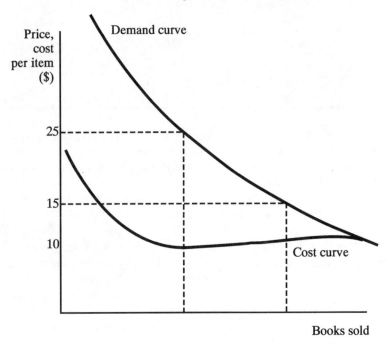

Figure 15.1   Demand and cost curves for mail order books

books, the publisher could get the overall per book cost (advertising, printing, fulfilment, postage, and so forth) down from $10 to $7.50, it would pay him to sell the book for $15. How could he reduce his costs? The biggest possible cost-cutting measure would be from the book printer. Traditionally, printers offer a substantial discount for bulk orders.

The other important factor is the value of the mailing list of book buyers. Most mail order firms rent their mailing lists for substantial added revenue. Suppose, for example, that the list can be rented for $100 per thousand names. If the entire list is rented once a week, total list rental income would be $520 000 if the list includes 100 000 names and $1 040 000 for a list of 200 000 names. Assuming the cost of advertising and renting the list was $200 000 a year, the income statement for the company would appear as in Table 15.2.

Thus, we can see how valuable a mailing list can be. In fact, the mailing list may be so valuable that many mail order firms promote their products as a 'loss leader' so that the rental income from the mailing list represents their entire profit.

Table 15.2   Book profit with a mailing list

For $25 book		For $15 book	
Gross revenues	$3.02 million	Gross revenues	$4.04 million
Gross costs	$1.20 million	Gross costs	$2.20 million
Total profit	$1.82 million	Total profit	$1.84 million

Add in the possible economies of scale by printing 200 000 instead of only 100 000 books, and the mail order firm might be more profitable by pricing the book at $15 instead of at $25.

In sum, a mail order outfit needs to take into account a wide variety of choices in order to maximize its profits, including retail prices, economies of scale, fixed and variable costs, the value of its mailing list, and advertising techniques. It is also worth noting that a mail order business is one of the few to be able to test a wide variety of prices and products, and thus to determine the varying elasticity along the entire demand curve.

M.S.

16.   The businessman's query

'An upward-sloping supply curve doesn't make sense in my business. All I know is that if I raise my prices, revenues don't go up, they go down. I don't sell more products, I sell less.' Can you straighten out this business-man's thinking?

The businessman's comment is a common example of confusing the supply curve with the demand curve. In fact, changing prices can make revenues go up or down, but the more salient issue is, what happens to profits?

Let's suppose this business (called the Custom Shirt Co., owned and operated by Mr Shirtsleeve) sells custom-made shirts in Manhattan, and his supply and demand situation looks as in Figure 16.1. In this

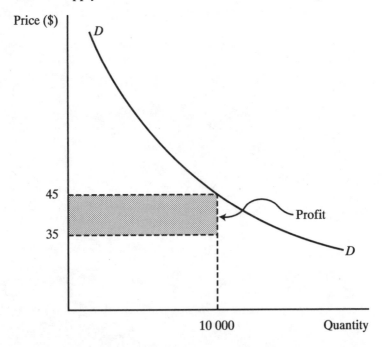

Figure 16.1   Equilibrium in the shirt market

case, the Custom Shirt Co. is in equilibrium. Last year Mr Shirtsleeve sold approximately 10 000 shirts at $45 each, for a gross revenue of $450 000 and a profit of $100 000 (the cost to produce each shirt is around $35). There is no backlog or inventory beyond the normal levels.

Now suppose he hires Dr Ivory, an economist, who tells Mr Shirtsleeve that his marketing studies indicate that the demand curve for his custom-made shirts is 'inelastic' and that he should raise his prices to maximize profits. 'Your shirts have brand-name value', Dr Ivory explains. 'I have no doubt that most of your customers would be willing to pay substantially more for your tailor-made shirts. So long as the percentage rise in price is greater than the percentage fall in shirt orders, your revenues will increase.' Mr Shirtsleeve is convinced and raises his shirt prices to $60 each. The next year, the Custom Shirt Co. sells only 7000 shirts, for a gross revenue of $420 000, slightly less than the previous year's sales. Apparently, Dr Ivory's research was wrong – the demand curve above $45 is elastic, not inelastic.

However, suppose the cost to produce each shirt is now $40, up from $35 due to fixed costs. His total profit for the year is $140 000, substantially more than the previous year. Dr Ivory may have been wrong

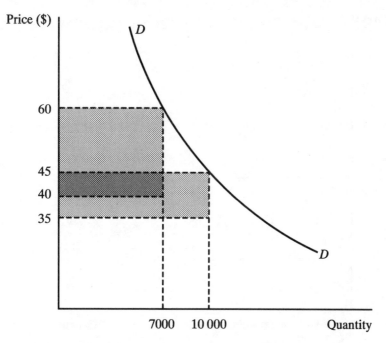

Figure 16.2 Increased profitability by raising prices

about the elasticity of demand for Mr Shirtsleeve's shirts, but his recommendation to raise prices appears to be a good one. Sales are down, gross revenues are down, but profits are up! Figure 16.2 demonstrates the improved profit picture for the Custom Shirt Co.

There are other cases where a business may want to raise prices. Take another possible situation facing the Custom Shirt Co. We noted that in the latest year, Mr Shirtsleeve raised his price to $60 per shirt, sold 7000 shirts for a gross revenue of $420 000 and made a profit of $140 000 (average cost for making a shirt is around $40). Now suppose in the next year, the nation suffers a recession and Mr Shirtsleeve sees a decided decline in shirt sales from 7000 to 6000. Gross revenues fall to $360 000, and with average costs rising to $45 a shirt, profits decline sharply from $140 000 to $90 000. What should he do?

Mr Shirtsleeve is tempted to raise his prices in an attempt to recoup his profits. He consults Dr Ivory, who warns the shirtmaker that his ploy may backfire. 'It might be better to lower prices', Dr Ivory counsels, 'not raise them.' He draws a diagram on the blackboard showing that the recession has caused the demand curve to shift downward, as shown in Figure 16.3. But Mr Shirtsleeve refuses to listen and raises his

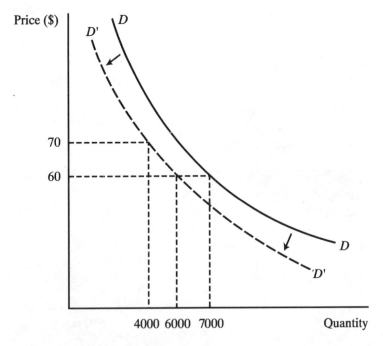

Figure 16.3 Fall in demand during a recession

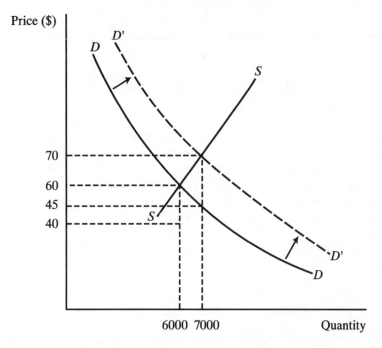

Figure 16.4   Upward-sloping supply curve for shirts

prices to $70. 'It worked last time, maybe it will work this time', he declares.

But the economist is proven right. In the next year, sales fall from 6000 shirts to 4000 shirts for a gross revenue of $280 000, and with an average cost of $50 a shirt, the total profit is only $80 000. The results confirm the businessman's original statement, 'All I know is that when I raise prices, revenues don't go up, they go down.' Consequently, Mr Shirtsleeve drops his price back down to $60 a shirt.

However, there is a third scenario in which Mr Shirtsleeve can have his cake and eat it too. Suppose the recession ends and demand for his custom-made shirts increases. The next year he raises his shirt price to $70 each, and he sells 7000 shirts, for a gross revenue of $490 000. As we can see from Figure 16.4, with higher volume, his average cost drops to $45 a shirt, for a total profit of $175 000. Mr Shirtsleeve is elated by discovering, finally, an upward-sloping supply curve!

M.S.

17. Are teachers underpaid?

Outstanding athletes such as Michael Jordan and Wayne Gretsky and famous movie stars and entertainers such as John Travolta and Garth Brooks earn multimillion-dollar annual incomes while the very best teachers earn considerably less. Were a survey to be taken most people would surely agree with the proposition that 'education is more important than entertainment'. Are teachers underpaid?

The question seems to suggest that people's behaviour and expressed attitudes are inconsistent or else the market system generates perverse relative wages. There are several aspects to resolving this puzzle.

In well-functioning market-oriented societies the wages for entertainers, in this case artistic performers, and athletes, and for teachers are set primarily by the intersection of supply and demand. When a worker offers her labour services for hire she normally wants to be paid more to work more hours since she is giving up time that could be devoted to non-work activities, called leisure. Consequently, the quantity of labour offered in the market rises as the wage rate rises. In contrast, labour demand slopes downward, reflecting the fact that the first units of labour hired are more productive for the buyer than the last units hired because of the law of diminishing returns. So, given demand for a type of labour, the lower the supply of labour, the higher the wage will be, other things being equal. Or, given supply, the greater the demand for labour, the higher the wage will be, other things being equal. Because of the relative scarcity of top entertainers relative to master teachers, wage rates are lower for the latter in the USA. So if we accept a market-oriented society as desirable, one could reasonably argue that we should accept the relative incomes generated by that market. Of course, this primer on supply and demand does not answer the question posed. We need to go further behind the market determination of wages to address the puzzle more fully.

The demand for any input such as a raw material, capital equipment or labour is a *derived demand*. This means that it is ultimately the monetary value of the output produced that determines the demand for an input. What is the monetary value of the output that labour produces? For factory and office workers it is the value of the good or service that is sold. Their wages, in well-functioning markets, can be expected to reflect the extra value of the goods and services which they produce – their productivity combined with their work–leisure tradeoff. If demand for the products they produce rises, so will the demand for their services and so will their wage rate. Wages (and salaries) are determined primarily by the interaction of labour supply and the derived labour demand. But wages are set at the margin where labour is hired. It is the satisfaction of labour and labour productivity for business of the *last* labourers hired that sets wage rates, not total satisfaction of labour or total productivity of labour. This means that even though citizens agree that education is qualitatively more important than entertainment and may in fact have more total productivity and total labour satisfaction associated with it, the market price does not reflect this fact. It instead reflects the value of the last units hired, and since the market has determined that there are fewer units of top entertainers relative to master teachers, relative to the demand for each, the wages of top entertainers are much higher than those of master teachers.

But this explanation suggests a further query. Why are the relative supply and demand curves for entertainers and teachers such that higher wages are generated for the former? To answer this we need to inquire into the 'other things being equal' assumption used to generate the explanation. Both labour demand and labour supply curves are conceived under the assumption that 'tastes' are constant. Should 'tastes' change, the curves are likely to shift significantly, giving very different monetary values for different kinds of labour. What are 'tastes'? Tastes derive from the social values of a society, and these are institutionalized in the norms and laws that define a culture and which affect the way information is filtered and processed by individuals in society. A market-oriented society that places a higher social value on entertainment activities will reveal this both by a greater monetary demand for sports and entertainment and higher salaries for those who provide them. While only $8 billion was spent on motion picture, theatre and spectator sports admissions compared to $528 billion spent on private and public education in 1992 (US Department of Commerce, 1995: 229, 253, 586), these figures conceal a great deal of the economic reality for teachers, and for entertainers. Much of the income received by athletes and artistic performers comes from TV and radio broadcast rights, and advertising and tie-in deals with products, so this figure seriously understates their economic importance. Also, many more people are involved in delivering educational services than in providing spectator sports, theatre and motion picture performances. There were almost 4 million teachers employed in 1994 while less than 200 000 athletes, actors and directors were employed (US Department of Commerce, 1995). These data are not detailed enough to demonstrate convincingly that entertainment values dominate educational values, but we can hypothesize what they would imply. A high aggregate value placed on sports and entertainment by US society will be reflected in wages paid to the types of labour that produce entertainment. Were US citizenry to decide that they wanted to spend relatively more on education (publicly and privately), the values of resources that produce education would likewise increase. This might involve a basic change in social values, which tend to change slowly and for reasons we do not understand very well. This is the reason why most economic analyses hold 'tastes' constant.

Clearly, supply and demand and their basic dependence on the social values of US culture may provide a major reason for the much higher salary of Michael Jordan compared to Eddie Fyer, an extraordinary teacher. And in a significant sense, teachers as a group are getting paid what they are worth, based on the values society holds as reflected in the interaction of supply and demand curves. However, average teacher salaries may not be too much different from what athletes and artistic performers earn on the average. There are many minor league athletes and unheard-of artistic performers who earn wages below those of even novice teachers. What is different about the two markets is the far greater disparity in salaries within the athletic and entertainment professions compared to those in teaching. The great disparity in salaries between top athletes and master teachers may have as much to do with the nature of the market for teachers as it does with the social values of society. Once we take this into account, we may be more reluctant to assume that the reason Garth Brooks makes more income than Eddie Fyer is that Garth Brooks is relatively more scarce.

Since the demand for labour is a derived demand, productivity is the measure used to determine how much the buyer or customer is willing to pay. The most common measure of productivity is output per person hour. The productivity of a great athlete such as Michael Jordan or a top artistic performer such as Garth Brooks can easily be evaluated by the extra gate receipts and media revenue their individual presence and performance generate. Indeed, determining this is a primary function of their agents. The great difference in salaries between average and top athletes and entertainers testifies to this fact. Determining the market value of master teachers such as Eddie Fyer is not so easily done.

Teaching is not in demand solely for the purpose of giving students information and skills to earn more income, but also reflects a strong interest that students should learn values thought worthy in a society, such as honesty, curiosity, and effective interaction with others. These values are not necessarily monetary in character. Greater honesty, curiosity, and social development translate only very crudely if at all into a higher lifetime income, and their acquisition is deemed laudable because citizens with these values make for a more desirable community, only one dimension of which is greater affluence. In fact the respect a community gives to teachers may well reflect its collective assessment of how well students are perceived to be learning the unmeasurable amalgamation of skills, information and values that teachers are teaching. Assessing whether teachers are paid what they are socially worth with reference to their teaching these non-monetary values is difficult since the level of respect accorded teachers is a community value, a broad brush that touches all teachers without differentiating any of them. The level of respect that teachers in general receive from different people in the community most certainly both overvalues and undervalues many teachers individually in terms of teacher quality since this cannot be individually assessed.

But how about the dimension of learning, information and skills, that is more closely related to market wages? One output teachers produce, student learning of information and skills, is valued in the market in the form of demand for students as workers. More learning of skills and information often translates into higher salaries and ultimately into higher lifetime earnings. So market demand for teachers is derived from the derived demand for students as workers. However, the contribution that an individual teacher makes to student learning of information and skills is very difficult to measure. Even if we could measure student learning, the translation of this learning input to the product the student produces as a worker is even more difficult to measure. Learning by an individual student is produced collectively by student ability, motivation, and the school system – of which an individual teacher is but a part. And identifying the components of this learning with components of a wage rate is a daunting task. None of this information is available to the labour market nor is it generated by the labour market itself. The market pricing of teachers reflects this.

Relative teaching wages do not correlate with the relative skills and information a student learns nor with the relative wages a student receives in the job market. Rather market wages of teachers in public schools are shaped more by the custom (and sometimes enforced by unions) of keeping them similar, even in private schools, except for easily measurable differences such as experience and education level attained. Consequently, teaching wages have a much narrower range than we see for athletes and artistic performers. Teacher salaries make very little distinction between outstanding teachers, average teachers, and weak teachers, because the demand for and supply of teachers does not differentiate teacher quality very well. The lack of information about teacher quality, and the inability of the market to generate this information, means that the demand for teachers is rather homogeneous. The market price then reflects the demand value of the last of a large number of undifferentiated teachers hired, and this homogeneous wage will be much lower than it would be for outstanding teachers if teacher quality could be differentiated by the market. The essential point is not that teacher quality is very similar, but rather that despite great dissimilarities, the market does not have enough information to reveal this. To put it differently, for teachers the market functions inefficiently, and the wage rate does not perform its rationing function. Hypothetically, if Eddie Fyer's contribution to an individual's skills and information could be determined by the market, and if Eddie commanded an audience similar to that of John Travolta or Wayne Gretsky, he might well be making the same or more income than they do. This suggests the market may not be allocating labour resources as efficiently as it could. The absence of a well-functioning market for teachers because of information deficiencies inherent in the market implies a valid criticism of market-determined wages for teachers even within the context of accepting market-determined wages generally as a legitimate system for generating relative wages in a society. This criticism of the market can be generalized to include any productive factor for which the quality cannot be differentiated by the market price because of the market's inability to create or access the appropriate information.

So the criticism that many teachers do not get paid what they are monetarily worth is partly valid because the output produced – individual student learning – cannot be effectively priced by the market; nor can teaching input into that learning be adequately priced. The information to do so is neither generated in nor available to the market. By the same token, it is equally valid to point out that many teachers are being overpaid compared to what they would earn if the market were able to price individual teacher contributions to student learning. In effect, the inability of the market to price differential effects on student learning and translate this into differential income earned means that superior teachers are subsidizing inferior teachers. Many teachers are being underpaid, but many other teachers are being overpaid. This situation is likely to persist so long as the market is unable to generate or utilize the information needed to differentiate teacher quality.

Looking at college teacher salaries can provide some confirmation of this view. At the college level scholarship has been an additional and usually much more important consideration than teaching in measuring teacher quality. The scholarship output of an individual teacher is more quantitatively measurable (quantity and refereed quality of writings) than teaching quality. Scholarship benefits the higher education institution by enhancing its reputation. A more prestigious institution attracts a stronger and larger student body and more donations and foundation funds. Salaries are considerably more variable than at the public school level, and salaries of individual professors with the same rank can vary significantly even in the same field at the same school. With consulting and book contracts, a few top professors' incomes are in the seven-figure range.

Does this mean that were we able to identify individual teacher contributions to student lifetime income, some public school teachers would earn significantly more – salaries in the six- or even seven-figure range? Perhaps. Certainly, Eddie Fyer's salary would be much closer to that of Michael Jordan than it now is. But a caveat is in order here. A major purpose of public school education is the development of social values that do not clearly translate into higher income. Teachers who could be identified as successful in helping students achieve such values would earn greater individual respect but not necessarily greater income for these socially important but difficult-to-price social values.

In conclusion we can see that teachers in general might be receiving an average salary that reflects the societal values held by the populace. However, this would be only because the overpayment of salary to lower-quality teachers about equalled the underpayment of salaries to higher-quality teachers, a happenstance occurrence. More relevantly, the wages to individual teachers do not reflect their individual quality. Without sound information about actual student learning of skills, information and socially beneficent values and individual teacher contribution to this learning, this situation is likely to persist, and the salaries of teachers will continue to be rather homogeneous, both under-valuing and overvaluing many. Are teachers paid what they are worth to society? Probably not, but John Travolta may be.

K.C.T.

REFERENCE

US Department of Commerce (1995), *Statistical Abstract of the USA, 1995*.

18.   The pollution puzzle

A 'good' is something we desire to have while a 'bad' is something we want to get rid of. Pollution is a bad. Since pollution is a bad by definition, logic implies that we should eliminate it. Why don't we?

To address this question we need to address three issues: the relation between waste and pollution, the importance of human pollution, and the perspective adopted to understand the pollution problem. Having done this we can see why the pollution issue won't go away.

Pollution should not be confused with *waste*. The first law of thermo-dynamics – that matter can neither be created nor destroyed – guarantees that waste, once generated, will remain perpetually in a system in some form. The second law of thermodynamics – that all matter must degrade over time – guarantees that waste can never be totally converted into a non-waste form. Biologically, these laws mean that waste is a necessary product of the production and consumption activities of all living biological entities (Arms and Camp, 1987: 1004) and must return to the ecosystem to go through another cycle of pro-duction, consumption and waste. Biological processes necessarily produce waste, often an important nutrient resource within ecosystems. Most waste is recycled as biological systems are very efficient in con-verting waste into re-inputs. Thus waste seldom creates undesirable changes in biological systems. Consequently, pollution produced by non-human ecosystems is minimal and rarely problematic.

A typical biological definition of pollution is that it is 'an undesirable change in the physical, chemical, or biological characteristics of an ecosystem' (Arms and Camp, 1987: 1022). Such a definition clearly implies that pollution is a bad. Nonetheless, it is overly broad. It is too broad in that it allows resource use and natural processes to be included as pollution, which is not the concept of pollution people usually have in mind. Over-use of natural resources may be an environmental problem, but it seems best to call it 'excessive resource use' rather than pollution. Also, the nuclear forces within the earth and from the sun have produced volcanic eruptions, earthquakes, and severe weather events such as tornadoes and hurricanes since the earth was formed, and they generate waste which can significantly harm ecosystems. Generation of this kind of 'pollution' is natural in the sense that it occurs regularly, and humans do not have control over it. Of more interest to us is pollution generated by biological systems themselves, human and non-human.

The human economic system of production and consumption activities necessarily produces waste which, if not recycled, also returns to the ecosystem. Human-produced pollution results from the fact that modern industrial human production and consumption are not, unlike bees and flowers, biologically bound to any particular ecosystem relationship. Humans can choose to produce and consume food, clothing, shelter and other artifacts from a variety of existing ecosystems and in a variety of locations. The rapid development of industrialization compared with the slow development of ecosystems has meant that no integrated ecosystem has developed (and perhaps cannot develop) to deal with human-produced wastes on their massive scale. The consequent inability of the economic system or the surrounding ecosystems to recycle the waste produced from industrial processes has meant that undesirable changes occur to these systems. Let's develop a more specific and useful ecological definition of pollution. An ecological definition of pollution would be as follows: 'Pollution results when the outputs of the human system exceed the carrying capacity of a surrounding non-human ecosystem so that either system is made less ecologically productive.' This ecological definition is attractive because it: represents what most people have in mind in considering pollution as a 'bad', allows that some portion of human waste is not pollution, specifies 'undesirable' as exceeding the carrying capacity of human and non-human systems, and is measurable in principle. Using this perspective, all pollution should be eliminated.

This conception of pollution takes the perspective of the ecosystem as a whole as its reference point and is commonly employed by many environmentalists. The role of humans in the ecosystem is to avoid altering the productive capacity of a biological system, while non-human altering of that capacity is 'natural' and desirable. Adopting this conception reflects an important ideological belief that reducing current human material well-being to avoid damaging the productive capacity of an ecosystem is desirable. This conception also requires the identification of carrying capacity so that we can determine when it is exceeded. Economists use another approach to understanding pollution that is based on understanding its role in the economic system.

Economists commonly define pollution as a *negative externality*, an unbargained for cost imposed on someone else (Goodstein, 1995: 32). Smoke from a steel mill imposes costs on the community in the form of deterioration of human health and damage to painted houses and cars, among other things. If these costs are unaccounted for, then the private costs of steel production do not equal the social costs of steel production as is implicitly assumed in standard economic theory. Consequently, economic efficiency is not achieved. The existence of pollution externalities in production means that polluting firms are producing too much at prices that are too low. Resources are being devoted to the production of steel that could more efficiently be employed elsewhere in the economy. In effect, if the steel mill not now accounting for the costs of pollution does account for them, it will produce less output at a higher price.

The negative externality conception of pollution identifies waste as pollution when residuals from production or consumption impose a cost on someone. Thus it is measurable in principle and, if property rights are fully specified and complete, it can also be measured empirically. If property rights are not fully specified or complete, that fact often becomes the first step toward solving a pollution problem so that costs can be measured and attributed to someone. The economic goal is to maximize human material well-being to produce an economically efficient outcome. Pollution only exists if human property rights are affected negatively by human-produced waste. Property rights may inhere in environmental amenities such as clean air if society desires it. Nonetheless, the economic benefit of avoiding the extermination of a species, say a small fish, could be zero if it is not commercially used and if no one is willing to pay money to create private or public property rights in the fish.

As a negative externality, pollution generation imposes a cost on someone in the economic system. However, this does not mean that it is 'bad' enough to be completely eliminated. This is because the reduction of pollution is also costly, and costs of reducing it must be compared with the benefits of reducing it in order to maximize human material well-being. Economic efficiency requires that net benefits of pollution reduction be maximized (or the net costs be minimized).

Suppose that Figure 18.1 represents the pollution reduction consequences of reducing steel production for a given state of technology. The quantity of pollution reduction as a percentage is given on the horizontal axis, and the cost of pollution reduction per unit is given on the vertical axis. The shapes of the curves illustrate two important principles.

The declining marginal benefit (MB) reflects the diminishing marginal utility of pollution reduction past some point, the most important health and material benefits occurring with the earlier units of pollution

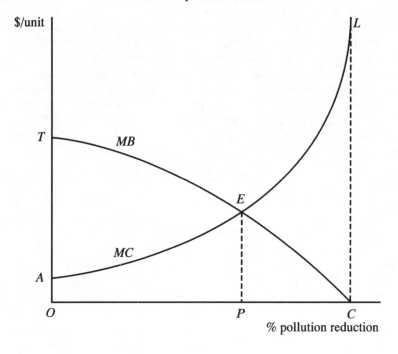

Figure 18.1   Benefits and costs of pollution reduction

reduction and increasingly smaller benefits occurring with later units when more of the pollution has already been reduced. At point *C* pollution reduction is 100 per cent, and the additional benefits of pollution reduction are obviously zero. Past that point, pollution is no longer a 'bad'.

The rising marginal cost curve (*MC*) implies that the first units of pollution cost little to eliminate but the cost per unit of pollution reduction rises as more is reduced. This reflects the law of diminishing marginal returns, the idea that it is less costly to eliminate the first units of pollution because simple measures are effective. As an increasing percentage of pollution is reduced, the methods to reduce it more become more expensive, costs rising exponentially past some point.

Economic efficiency requires that pollution reduction proceed until *MB* = *MC*. At this point material well-being is optimal since net benefits, $\Sigma (MB - MC)$ = area *EAT*, are maximized. That is, reducing pollution more than at point *P* would subtract from net benefits since *MC* > *MB* past that point, while reducing pollution by less than *P* would fail to maximize net benefits since *MB* > *MC* before that point. We can now solve the pollution puzzle, at least from a mainstream economic perspective.

Pollution is a negative externality, an unbargained-for cost imposed on someone else, and thus it creates a cost that would not exist were the polluting activity not undertaken. Negative externalities are 'bads'. However, reducing pollution that already exists uses up economic resources that could be used for other production, including reducing other forms of pollution. Consequently, economists weigh the economic costs against the economic benefits of reducing a given form of pollution to decide how much pollution to reduce. Efficient pollution reduction occurs where $MB = MC$ and this will seldom be at 100 per cent pollution reduction. Pollution reduction at point C in Figure 18.1 eliminates all the 'bad' pollution, but creates a misuse of resources in the sense that the market demands of people, valued by their dollar votes, are not being heeded. In fact in this example, production at point C is not only economically inefficient but even leads to a net absolute economic loss to society compared to permitting all pollution since the net costs, Σ $(MB - MC)$ = area ECL, at point C are greater than the net benefits at point O, Σ $(MB - MC)$ = area EAT.

The economic definition of pollution takes the perspective of the human economic system as a whole as its reference point, and the ecosystem is seen as a resource to be utilized to maximize human material well-being. Wastes which reduce the productive capacity of the ecosystem are not necessarily seen as pollution that should be eliminated if their costs of reduction are less than the benefits provided by exploiting an ecosystem. To eliminate such pollution would be 'unnatural' in the context of the economic efficiency goal. Adopting this conception implies an important ideological belief that the operation of markets with complete and well-defined property rights will create the incentives and changes in economic variables needed to sustain and maximize future human material well-being. This definition also requires the identification of environmental costs and benefits of pollution so that we can determine the optimal level of pollution.

Is pollution then an unalloyed bad? It is if you employ an ecological perspective on pollution, and it is not if you employ an economic perspective on pollution. However, in order to implement either view, the basic concepts must be measured. Identifying and measuring the carrying capacity of ecosystems is difficult and identifying the economic costs and benefits of pollution reduction measures is no less so. Some progress in generating these estimates has been achieved, but much more remains to be done. Consequently, those who employ these perspectives tend to rely on beliefs derived from the perspectives rather than evidence.

In terms of Figure 18.1, an environmentalist might argue that a point to the right of P, all the way up to C, is desirable if reducing pollution by more than P possibly continues to improve the productive capacity of the ecosystem. They would rely on the ecological definition of pollution that exceeding carrying capacity is the defining feature of pollution. They would argue that the biophysical principles of thermodynamics and carrying capacity should dominate the economic principles of the economic efficiency of market allocation. Therefore, the ecosystem costs of exceeding the unknown carrying capacity of the environment are not worth the risks. They would downplay the economic perspective by noting that damaging ecosystem productivity raises future costs of reducing pollution much higher than currently, as known resources become more costly. They would also note that the free resource services of clean air and water, now being degraded by pollution, create future unknown economic costs to be reckoned with.

In contrast, mainstream economists adopt the negative externality conception of pollution, because pollution becomes explainable within an economic framework. While the laws of thermodynamics and the carrying capacity concept may hold, the effects of their operation on the ecosystem do not seem as problematic within a relevant time frame. The creation of property rights that incorporate pollution costs, say through marketable permits or pollution taxes, imply higher prices for polluting products. These higher prices create incentives to reduce their production and provide material incentives to switch to non-polluting products. They also provide incentives to recycle and to develop new methods for production that are less polluting, thus overcoming the law of diminishing returns associated with any given production process. The market contains needed feedbacks to prevent exceeding the economically relevant carrying capacity of the environment. Such economists would stress the deleterious effects of stymying the desire for material well-being as the driving force of the economic system since new resources are found and new technology is developed as a result of the desire for material betterment. Eventually, when the dollar votes of buyers are revealed and the technological capabilities of suppliers warrant it, a market economic system creates the production methods and consumption patterns that generate less polluting waste.

While almost everyone agrees that pollution is a bad, we have difficulty determining when waste, a natural process, becomes pollution and measuring its effects on the ecosystem and the economy. Consequently, a greater faith in biophysical principles or economic markets not only shapes one's perception of pollution but also the urgency with which it should be addressed. Unless our ability to measure carrying capacity and economic benefits and costs improves significantly, this ideological conflict is likely to continue to dominate the pollution issue.

K.C.T.

REFERENCES

Arms, Karen and Pamela S. Camp (1987), *Biology*, 3rd edn, New York: Saunders College Publishing.
Goodstein, Eban S. (1995), *Economics and the Environment*, Englewood Cliffs, New Jersey: Prentice-Hall.

19.   Are market wages fair?

In a market, the wages a person earns tend to reflect that person's productivity. More work effort implies greater worker productivity and this in turn implies higher worker wages. Economic systems that do not constrain this process have higher income inequality than systems that constrain it. Is this then a fair way to determine wages?

'Fairness' can be a slippery concept, and there are many ways to approach it, ranging from the concrete to the abstract. Let's adopt a concrete conception that what is fair is what most people want as reflected in the relatively permanent choices they actually make, both economically and politically. This is an approach that economists appreciate, resting as it does on individual choice.

In a market-oriented society, wages and salaries are determined primarily by the interaction of labour supply and labour demand. The downward-sloping demand for labour reflects the fact that the first units of labour hired are more valuable to the firm than the last units hired. But as the resolution of Adam Smith's diamond–water paradox reveals, market-determined prices reflect the value of labour at the margin, the last unit hired. So the greater the supply of labour, the lower the wage, other things being equal. Since the demand for any input such as labour is a derived demand, it is ultimately the monetary value of the output produced that determines the demand for labour. Equally skilled wage-earners who work in a firm receive a wage that reflects the monetary contribution they collectively make to the firm. Wages thus tend to reflect the marginal productivity of the work done.

The market has been legitimized as the basic mechanism for allocating resources and determining incomes in the USA. We know this because politically, US citizens have never voted to change fundamentally the market determination of wages and salaries, say by voting on wage schedules for jobs. Nor have we developed many private institutions, other than labour unions, that provide alternative methods for determining salaries, such as wage boards or worker-owned firms. In a market-oriented economic system wages are certain to be unequal because the relative demand and supply of skills differs substantially, and this fundamental fact of the market seems to be accepted by most people. Consequently, there is significant evidence that most people do not in fact view differential salaries in general as grossly unfair, at least not so much as to change the nature of the economic system. Labour unions have been important as a means to keep their workers' wages higher, but part of their political justification has been that the monopoly power of firms has kept wages below what a competitive market would have set. In recent years the influence and membership of labour unions has declined markedly in the USA. Nonetheless, despite the acceptance of the market as the basic institution for wage determination, the market determination of wages in the USA and all high-income countries is supplemented by public institutions that alter this process. Why countries have done this has a great deal to do with wage fairness.

Most people in the USA and other high-income countries agree that individual choices should be the primary determinant of a person's economic involvement – as buyers and sellers of goods and services and as buyers and sellers of owned resources, including one's labour. They disagree on how much individual choice an individual actually has. Some people would argue that it is unfair that a person's income should depend solely on the impersonal forces of the market when much of the supply of labour brought to the market is not under the control of the wage-earner. This is a relevant argument since main-stream economic models assume that individual choice dominates decision making, subject to the non-choice elements acting only as boundary constraints. Moreover, such constraints can often be eliminated by appropriate behaviour by an individual. In such an economic system, fairness depends on the ability of individuals to control their market prospects for wages and salaries. In order to address this view of fairness we need to determine what elements at the level of the individual contribute to the wage and salary earned in a market-oriented society.

A number of elements that shape a person's earnings come to mind: innate ability (cognitive, emotional and other intelligences), strong motivation (including materialistic orientation and willingness to take risks and deal with uncertainty), appropriate knowledge (about ideas, people, things, processes), ownership or control of resources, good luck, a social climate that promotes material betterment (strong property rights structure, societal attitudes that legitimize and promote the search for material betterment) and the immediate circumstances of one's working environment. Some of these elements cannot be said to be chosen individually because the individual has limited or no control over them: innate ability, luck and social climate. The rest remain at least partially under the control of the individual decision maker except to the extent that all of them may depend somewhat on a person's experiences as a child, during which time decision-making authority is limited.

Economists simplify analysis by viewing a worker's wage as derived primarily from their productivity, commonly measured by output per person hour. This captures the economic impact of the immediate work environment. However, it does not help us understand the distinction between choice and non-choice factors that resulted in the immediate work experience. Choice of immediate work environment is generated partially by the elements under individual control, but it also results from non-choice elements that shaped the choice of the work environment itself. The relative importance of choice and non-choice elements depends on an individual's specific circumstances that led up to the immediate work environment. And once the immediate work environment is chosen, many of the determinants of a worker's productivity are not predictable by or under the control of the worker. These include such events as the physical capital that a worker has to use, the structure of the workplace, and management attitudes.

The fact is that one's wage, and income generally, depends both on the choices one makes and non-choice elements, while the relative influence of each on any individual remains uncertain. This inherent uncertainty makes the choice issue problematic as it bears on fairness. Allowing earnings to depend solely on a system, the market, that generates efficient outcomes under the assumption that only people's individual choices are the guiding principle is clearly unfair if wages depend importantly on non-choice elements. Non-choice elements could include innate ability such as high or low cognitive intelligence, luck in the form of being born the son of the president of a corporation or a drug addict, and social climate such as favouring certain physical characteristics or racial discrimination. By contrast, allowing earnings to be determined by a non-market system, such as government-determined wage schedules, is also unfair unless non-choice elements dominate the wage one receives. It is clear that US citizens have rejected the latter option, a market socialist system. It is equally clear that they have rejected a purely market system for the determination of wages.

Analysis of the uncertain combination of individual choice and non-choice elements leads to the supposition that people will choose a market system that is socially embedded in public institutions that shape and constrain the market wage determination process. In fact this is the kind of economic system the citizens of a variety of high-income countries have chosen. Broad social welfare systems have been created in many market-oriented high-income economies despite their varying social philosophies (McKenzie and Tullock, 1989: 208). In many high-income countries levels of government have developed programmes and rules that help shape the market determination of incomes under a rationale of greater fairness. In the USA these include such programmes as progressive income tax; occupational, health and safety rules; workmen's compensation, minimum wage legislation, Medicare, Medicaid and food stamps; agricultural subsidies, housing subsidies, and zoning laws. All countries have also used the strong power of governments to shape and guide both production and income distribution. The almost universal existence of mixed economies of markets and government is the recognition at the system level that, at the level of the individual, both choice and non-choice elements determine one's livelihood in ways that are difficult to determine and that people understand this. Even so, the mix of the market process with government institutions varies from country to country, partly because of the different emphases given to economic goals.

Societies such as the USA, whose citizens have emphasized market choice over non-choice elements, let market outcomes dominate relative income issues and consequently have greater variation in wages and salaries than countries such as Germany that place greater emphasis on non-choice elements that affect individual choice. Other outcomes are inherent in these societal choices. A more choice-oriented society such as the USA will create more individual opportunity for great individual economic success and will tend to have a lower unemployment rate. A less choice-oriented society such as Germany will tend to have a greater sense of community, less likelihood of individual economic failure, and a higher unemployment rate. Which is fairer?

A too facile answer might seem to be that it depends on whether you are a German or a US citizen. But in fact that is the best answer, given our choice of a 'fairness' concept. Fairness, unlike productivity, is solely a qualitative concept. Citizens in a democracy will not tolerate for long an economic system that they regard as 'unfair'. For the system to survive, it will have to be altered. Besides, citizens' views about economic fairness are not static. They can change over time. As sentiment within a country about the relative importance of choice and non-choice elements in income determination alters over time, we would expect the nature and strength of the social institutions in which the market process is embedded to change accordingly. Were this not to happen, it would be unfair.

K.C.T.

REFERENCES

Gardner, Howard (1983), *Frames of Mind: The Theory of Multiple Intelligences*,
New York: Basic Books.

McKenzie, Richard B. and Gordon Tullock (1989), *The Best of the New World
of Economics*, 5th edn, Homewood, Illinois: Irwin, ch. 14.

20. The highly valued occupation nobody wants

A survey of college students found that farming was ranked the number one most important occupation in the world. Yet less than 1 per cent of the students wanted to be farmers. How do you explain this apparently irrational response?

It may not be as irrational as you think. Students are quite right in concluding that farming is an extremely important occupation, given food's critical role in the survival of the human species. Thus, total utility of agriculture is by nature extremely high. But, as we demonstrated in the diamond–water paradox (2), marginal utility may be considerably less than total utility.

The field of agriculture has become so capital-intensive (due to mechanical power, machinery and chemical advances) that less and less labour is needed to produce agricultural commodities. Hence the farm population has fallen. Even as the population of the USA has grown, farm population has gradually declined from 30 million to less than 10 million over the past century. American agriculture has suffered from chronic labour surplus and a dramatic shift toward agribusiness. Not surprisingly, the number of students majoring in agricultural economics has declined sharply during the postwar period (Fox, 1987: 60). Table 20.1 indicates the dramatic change in US agriculture since 1870.

Table 20.1 Farming and the transformation of America

	1870	1989
Percentage of income spent on food	70%	20%
Percentage of workers in agriculture	50%	3%
Percentage urbanized	40%	74%

In sum, the world's ability to produce relatively abundant amounts of agricultural products has sharply reduced the number of people in farming. Capital advances have sharply reduced the need for farm labour. As the theory of marginal utility suggests, once our most urgent wants are satisfied (food), we can devote more of our resources and work to less urgent needs.

The above confirms Engel's Law, named after Ernst Engel (1821–96), a Prussian statistician who calculated the income elasticity of food and found it be less than one. As income increases, households tend to spend less of their budget on food (Houthakker, 1987: 144).

M.S.

REFERENCES

Boserup, E. (1987), 'Agricultural growth and population change', *The New Palgrave*, **1**, 62–8. New York: Macmillan.

Fox, Karl A. (1987), 'Agricultural economics', *The New Palgrave*, **1**, New York: Macmillan, 55–62.

Houthakker, H. S. (1987), 'Engel's Law', *The New Palgrave*, **2**, New York: Macmillan, 143–4.

Lebergott, Stanley (1993), *Pursuing Happiness: American Consumers in the Twentieth Century*, Princeton, New Jersey: Princeton University Press.

Schultz, T. W. (1964), *Transforming Traditional Agriculture*, New Haven, Connecticut: Yale University Press.

21. The stock market puzzler

Louis Bachelier, a French mathematician and stock market observer, wrote in his 1900 dissertation, 'Theory of Speculation': 'It seems that the market, the aggregate of speculators, at a given instant can believe in neither a market rise nor a market fall, since, for each quoted price, there are as many buyers as sellers' (Bernstein, 1992: 20). Therefore, according to Bachelier's logic, the stock market can never rise or fall, but must stand still. How do you explain why the stock market moves, sometimes dramatically, given that for every buyer there is a willing seller?

Louis Bachelier, who studied speculative prices at the turn of the twentieth century, is considered by some financial economists to be the father of the efficient market theory and the random walk hypothesis. He was the first to suggest that prices in capital markets are impossible to predict. 'The mathematical expectation of the speculator is zero', he declared (Bernstein, 1992: 21). In other words, the probabilities are 50 per cent that a price will rise and 50 per cent that it will fall.

It is true, of course, that for every buyer there is a seller in the stock and commodity markets. This elementary fact is often forgotten during periods of crisis in the market. 'Everyone's selling!' the broker says during a crash. 'Everyone's buying!' the broker says during a super bull market. Yet there must be selling when another investor is buying, and vice versa. The exchange cannot record a sale of X number of shares or Y number of contracts without a willing buyer and seller getting together and agreeing on one price.

But it is also important to note that stock prices listed in the financial pages are always historical, after the fact. It says nothing about the number of buyers and sellers before the transactions take place, which can differ considerably from the previous transaction. Revealed sales are not the same as desired sales. This salient truth is left out of the Bachelier equation.

A posteriori, after the trade, there is only one possibility – the number of purchases equals the number of sales. But *a priori*, before the sale, there are three possibilities. First, there can be more buyers than sellers (or, to be technically more accurate, more desired purchases than desired sales), thereby putting upward pressure on the price. Second, there can be an equal number of bids and offers, thereby maintaining the status quo price. And third, there can be more seller than buyers, thereby putting downward pressure on prices.

Whenever the number of desired purchases differs from the number of desired sales, the market makers are under pressure to adjust the price either up or down. And that's how stock, commodity and currency prices are determined.

Speculators and financial analysts who are alert to changes in investment sentiment and trading pressures can anticipate movements in prices and thereby profit accordingly. For these speculator–entrepreneurs, the probability of the prices of capital assets moving up or down can be fairly high, sometimes far above the 50 per cent chance that Bachelier suggested. The number of speculator–entrepreneurs having this unique ability to foresee market trends and outperform the averages is relatively small, however (Malkiel, 1990; Skousen, 1992).

M.S.

REFERENCES

Bernstein, Peter L. (1992), *Capital Ideas: The Improbable Origins of Modern Wall Street*, New York: Free Press.

Malkiel, Burton G. (1990), *A Random Walk Down Wall Street*, 5th edn, New York: W. W. Norton.

Skousen, Mark (1992), 'The Efficient Market Theory: Can You Beat the Market?', *The Investor's Bible: Mark Skousen's Principles of Investment*, Potomac, Maryland: Phillips Publishing.

22. Apples and the Alchian–Allen theorem

In Washington state, it is casually observed that the best Washington delicious apples are exported out of the state. This contradicts common sense. Shouldn't the best apples be found where they are produced?

The delicious apple debate raises an issue that has become known as the 'Alchian–Allen theorem'. According to Armen A. Alchian and William R. Allen, when the same fixed cost is added to the price of two similar goods, the effect will be to raise the *relative* consumption of the higher-quality or premium good. Hence higher-quality goods are likely to be exported (Alchian and Allen, 1972: 70–71).

This Alchian–Allen effect has been noted in many markets – oranges and grapes in California, leather goods in Italy, French wines, Texas steaks, Colombian coffee, Idaho potatoes, Hawaiian pineapples, Florida oranges and Washington apples. Alchian and Allen extend the argument even further:

> Why do Asians import disproportionately more expensive American cars rather than cheaper models? Why are 'luxuries' disproportionately represented in international trade? Why do young parents go to expensive plays rather than movies *relatively* more often than do young couples without children? Why are 'seconds' more heavily consumed near the place of manufacture than further away? (Alchian and Allen, 1972: 71).

The issue germinated when Alchian and Allen responded to a letter to the editor in the *Seattle Times* (19 October 1975) from an irate consumer complaining that he couldn't get any quality apples in a local grocery store. The consumer wrote:

> Why are Washington apples in local markets so small and old-looking? Recently, some apple-picking friends brought some apples they had just picked, and they were at least four times the size of those available for sale here. Where do these big Delicious apples go? Are they shipped to Europe, to the East or can they be bought here in Seattle? Signed, M.W.P.

Alchian and Allen responded as follows:

Regarding M.W.P.'s complaint that all the good apples were being shipped to the East, you might be interested to know that 'shipping the good apples out' has been a favorite classroom and exam question in the economics department at U.W. for many years. It is a real phenomenon, easily explained: Suppose, for example, a 'good' apple costs 10 cents and a 'poor' apple 5 cents locally. Then, since the decision to eat one good apple costs the same as eating two poor apples, we can say that a good apple in essence 'costs' two poor apples. Two good apples cost four poor apples. Suppose now that it costs 5 cents per apple (any apple) to ship apples East. Then, in the East, good apples will cost 15 cents each and poor ones 10 cents each. But now eating two good apples will cost three – not four poor apples. Though both prices are higher, good apples have become relatively cheaper, and a higher percentage of good apples will be consumed in the East than here. It is no conspiracy – just the [law of demand]. (Quoted in Borcherding and Silberberg, 1978: 131–2)

Since then, John Gould and Joel Segall have challenged the Alchian–Allen theorem, asking rhetorically, 'How often is it heard, for example, that the way to get really good farm produce is to drive out to the country and buy it at a roadside stand or that one must go to Maine to get truly delectable lobsters?' (Gould and Segall, 1968). However, as Borcherding and Silberberg respond, this criticism is unjustified. The Alchian–Allen theorem assumes no spoilage, ripening, or other quality changes in the goods en route to the final destination (Borcherding and Silberberg, 1978: 133).

John Umbeck extends the Alchian–Allen theorem to tax theory. What effect would a per unit tax have on liquor or cigarettes, for example? In the case of tobacco, it would 'lead to consumers buying more smoking minutes per pack' (Umbeck, 1980: 206). He suspects that increases in cigarette taxes have led to the introduction of king-size and super-king-size cigarettes.

Look at the effect of a unit tax of, say, $1 per bottle of liquor. The price of cheap wine like Tynderbird, Ripple or Boone's Farm would rise by a far greater percentage than the price of a rare $100 bottle of French wine.

What if the telephone company increases its installation charge per telephone? Fewer people will have phones, but 'those who do will use them more'. Similarly, 'if the fixed charge for making a local call on a pay telephone is increased, people will make fewer calls but will talk longer per call' (Umbeck, 1980: 206).

What about the possibility that out-of-state demand may be higher for imported goods? It's possible, respond Alchian and Allen, 'but then why are the oranges and grapes [from California] sold even in the poor districts of New York better than those sold in California?' (Alchian and Allen, 1972: 71).

In short, whenever a tax, transportation expense or other fixed cost is added to a variable cost of a product, the Alchian–Allen effect takes place: consumers tend to shift their tastes in favour of higher-quality products.

M.S.

REFERENCES

Alchian, Armen A. and William R. Allen (1972), *University Economics*, 3rd edn, Belmont, California: Wadsworth Publishing.

Borcherding, Thomas E. and Eugene Silberberg (1978), 'Shipping the Good Apples Out: The Alchian and Allen Theorem Reconsidered', *Journal of Political Economy*, February, 131–8.

Gould, John P. and Joel Segall (1968), 'The Substitution Effects of Transportation Costs', *Journal of Political Economy*, January/February, 130–37.

Kaempfer, William H. and Raymond T. Brastow (1985), 'The Effect of Unit Fees on the Consumption of Quality', *Economic Inquiry*, April, 341–8.

Landsburg, Steve (1995), *Price Theory and Applications*, 3rd edn, St Paul, Minnesota: West Publishing.

Umbeck, John (1980), 'Shipping the Good Apples Out: Some Ambiguities in the Interpretation of "Fixed Charge"', *Journal of Political Economy*, February, 199–208.

23. The perfect-market puzzle

In perfect financial markets, the prices of the assets are information-rich so that it is virtually impossible for any individual consistently to buy and sell a stock at a greater profit than the market average. The US financial market is often considered the best example of a perfect market. Yet millions of investors in the US financial market (and world markets) continually try to beat the market averages. Are financial markets very imperfect or are people very irrational?

Three main theories for the determination of stock prices have been developed, each having different implications for the perfection of the market and the rationality of individuals. In turn these imply strategies that people should employ to make money in the stock market. Virtually all the advice one hears regarding strategies to make money in the stock market is based on one of these three theories of stock price determination.

Fundamental theory, the oldest theory of stock market investing, motivates the behaviour of most investors in the USA. It says that there is an underlying or *intrinsic value* for a financial asset that depends on economic or market values. Intrinsic value can be said to equal expected earnings times the justified price/earnings (P/E) ratio (Kolb, 1992: 426). This is less helpful than it appears since a great deal goes into determining both of these variables. This is done by examining the 'fundamentals' of stocks – current and future estimated earnings and risk as determined by examining price/book value ratios, P/E ratios, earnings history, dividend yields, management philosophy and changes.

One determines the intrinsic value of a stock by working harder and smarter than others to acquire good information about individual stock prices and quality. A great deal of research on company performance is required, and successful investors are those who can consistently put this information together to determine intrinsic value. Market values may temporarily diverge but ultimately return to intrinsic values. Intrinsic values can change over time, but they do so slowly and predictably for those with the skill and good judgement to understand them. Market values may diverge temporarily from intrinsic values because of lags and noise.

Lags in information flow are a permanent feature of the market wherein new information is constantly entering the market and taking time to be understood and absorbed by market participants. Those market participants who more rapidly absorb this information make higher market profits than others who are slower to do so.

Market values also diverge from intrinsic values due to noise. Noise is distorted, imprecise or imperfect information about stock prices and quality. However, it is quickly dominated by intrinsic value as the market ultimately corrects for noise. Market participants who learn how to separate noise from true information make higher market profits than others.

Consequently, successful fundamental investors are those who correctly and quickly access market information and separate it from market noise or misinformation. Investors are not irrational but some are better informed than others. Fundamentalists believe that stock prices will revert to their fundamental values when information lags are closed and temporary noise in the market subsides. Markets are not informationally perfect, but they eventually move to equilibrium. Evidence supporting this theory would be the existence of individuals who consistently outperform the market by adopting a fundamental strategy.

Technical theory, sometimes called 'chartism', sees a short cut to the time-consuming approach of fundamental analysis. It is not necessary to pore over prospectuses and balance sheets of companies to find individual company diamonds in the rough; rather the past movement of stock prices in general can be understood as implying future movement of stock prices. Thus technical theory is primarily concerned with anticipating the price changes in the market as a whole, although it can be employed to select individual stocks.

Supply and demand determine the values of stocks in the market, but some of these forces are irrational. Thus, price trends develop that last for considerable periods of time, and technical indicators can reveal the start of a demand or supply shift in the market. Proper technics can permit you to act in the early stages of a shift because new information is only gradually absorbed in the market. There are a great many traditional technical indicators, but they can be seen as motivated by three approaches: act with market participants (i.e. follow the actions of the wise), act against most market participants (i.e. move contrary to the actions of the majority fools), act on perceived market regularities (i.e. look at past movements in stock prices). Follow-the-wise strategies include buying stocks when there are below-normal short sales by specialists or when advances minus declines become negative. Contrarian strategies include selling stocks short when the total volume of odd-lot sales is peaking, or buying stocks when mutual fund cash positions are peaking. Market regularity approaches include buying when the market breaks a psychological peak such as 4000 for the Dow or selling when the market goes below its previous low. A set of terms such as 'peaks', 'valleys' and 'breakout prices' has been developed to discern identifiable but hard-to-identify patterns. Technical theory sees some market participants as irrational and sees market outcomes as inefficient but predictable. Evidence supporting technical theory would be advice from technical investment advisors which, if followed, yielded a higher than average rate of return for a substantial time period. More recently, the use of sophisticated mathematical concepts and computer software has created new interest in what we shall call *technotechnical theory*. Technotechnical theory relies on the idea that patterns in the data are meaningful if an investor using that information could have made greater gains than the average investor. Data are mined to look for previously undiscovered patterns, and theoretical explanations come later. Rationales include the ideas that market traders are heterogeneous, having different goals, investment time horizons, and attitudes toward risk (*The Economist*, 1993). Thus the same data will rationally provide different information to different investors. In addition, investors may herd, adopting a belief about the market because they believe everyone else holds it. This combination of behaviours will, in the aggregate, produce stock price patterns, often discovered by various kinds of moving averages. Those clever enough to discover these patterns can make money in the stock market by using this information.

Efficient markets theory (EMT) is the newest of the three theories of investing. Developed in the 1960s, it has dominated academic research. Often ignored or disparaged on Wall Street in the past, EMT says that stock prices adjust rapidly to new information so that they fully reflect all the information that is known about a stock. It assumes that in the stock market many buyers and sellers are acting independently, and information comes to the market in random fashion that is not predictable either by looking at past stock market price patterns (as suggested by technical theory) or by looking at the financial details of individual companies (as suggested by fundamental theory). Since only unpredictable news can cause price changes, price changes must be unpredictable. An individual or portfolio manager cannot consistently outperform the stock market – as measured by some broad market aggregate such as the S&P 500 index in the USA. Beating the market in the short term is due to good luck only, a random result. The only way to get predictably higher returns on a stock portfolio is to take more risk (as measured by the variability in stock price over some defined time period), and the risk/return relationship is explainable by the capital asset pricing model (CAPM).

EMT is intellectually appealing to mainstream economists for two reasons. First, it provides the process by which the stock market moves toward equilibrium, and this supports the CAPM found to be of great use in finance. Second, it is a major extension of the logic of the neoclassical competitive market model of the individual firm and of rational expectations reasoning used increasingly in macroeconomics since the mid-1970s. It has gained a wide following in the economics profession, many of whose practitioners have used it to criticize much of the advice given by Wall Street and other investment advisors which is often based on the other two theories. In EMT market participants are very rational and market outcomes are always at or near equilibrium.

We can distinguish three versions of EMT which have different implications for all three stock market theories if they are true (Fama, 1976). Weak EMT sees prices as reflecting only historical data. Thus this version negates technical analysis but allows a role for fundamental analysis. Semi-strong EMT sees prices as reflecting both historical and publicly available information. Consequently, it negates both fundamental and technical analysis. Strong EMT sees stock prices as information-rich, containing all past and public information on the firm and its stock and including private information as well, such as that held by corporate leaders. It makes no concession to either of the other two theories and sees markets as always and everywhere efficient. While the strong version of EMT has not been supported because evidence indicates that corporate insiders and market specialists do earn above normal rates of return on stocks they own, both the semi-strong and weak versions of EMT were uniformly supported by a rich set of empirical research until the mid-1980s (Kolb, 1992: 545–96). Empirical evidence which supports weak and semi-strong EMT includes the inability of past stock prices (such as the S&P 500) statistically to predict current stock prices; there is evidence that a buy-and-hold strategy for a diversified array of stocks or buying a market index mutual fund has outperformed technical and fundamental stock strategies; and there is a lack of individuals and portfolio managers who have beaten the market consistently over a substantial time period.

Despite its academic prestige, evidence negating the semi-strong version of EMT has begun to accumulate during the last ten years. First, there have been a few portfolio managers, such as Peter Lynch and Warren Buffett, who have consistently outperformed the market for over ten years. Such evidence is not definitive since this could be a statistical anomaly; there are thousands of portfolio managers whose strategies are not objectively identifiable. Even with completely random stock picking, a few individual investors or advisors will end up in the tails of the rate of return distribution (i.e. be very unlucky or very lucky). By this criterion, the strategies of such lucky investors are no more useful than the strategy of the latest state lottery winner in picking 'his' number.

Of more importance is the statistical evidence for a number of results which are problematic for EMT. EMT implies that real stock prices are equal to the present value of their expected future dividends. For the stock market as a whole there is no evidence that stock price movements are followed by corresponding dividend movements (Shiller, 1981). Other evidence relates to effects which should not exist if EMT is correct. These include calendar effects such as strategies to buy in late December to catch the January effect, buying at the end of any month to catch the beginning-of-the-month effect, buying on Fridays, and buying before holidays (Thaler, 1992: 139–50). Additional evidence includes historically higher rates of return for buying small-firm stocks and buying on the basis of especially favourable quarterly earnings reports, the excess volatility of stock prices, and the mean reversion of stock prices (Kolb, 1992: 582–8). These empirical inconsistencies with EMT have prompted a very different approach to understanding stock price changes that involves *noise traders*.

Noise trading is buying or selling securities on the basis of something other than fundamentals. Noise traders, in contrast to information traders, are irrational in that they incorrectly process market information, trading on the basis of noise. EMT assumes either no existence of noise traders or, like fundamental theory, the temporary existence of noise traders as rational arbitrageurs reap gains at their expense and drive them out of the market. Technical theory requires substantial noise trading, enough so that fundamentals are swamped and prediction by fundamentals is not possible. However, technical theorists believe that prediction is still possible by discerning past patterns in aggregate stock prices. These patterns reveal predictable changes in investor sentiment or psychology which is an important mover of stock prices, particularly in the short run. We have seen that there is no evidence to support the technical theory's version of market noise, but that does not negate other conceptions of market noise behaviour.

US financial markets are very competitive. There are many buyers and sellers acting relatively independently, products are homogeneous (shares of a given company are identical), financial resources are very mobile and entry and exit are easy. Consequently, information is processed rapidly, and this is reflected in prices. Lags in information flows are short and by themselves do not allow for much differential profit by knowledgeable investors. However, noise may be a much more serious problem than presumed by the efficient markets theory because there are strong economic incentives to generate noise, and it is difficult for investors to separate noise from information. As a consequence stock markets are competitive but not very efficient in terms of information processing and may not reach equilibrium easily if at all.

Robert Shiller (1993) has argued that existing evidence does not negate the belief that the US stock market is subject to social influences and fads in investing. The average investor has no generally accepted theory of stock market investing to believe in, nor does he have a way to separate noise from information when both are offered by investment advisors. Consequently he is faced with a great deal of uncertainty in making investment choices. Citing social psychology literature, Shiller argues that in such an environment investors are especially susceptible to social influences and group pressure and this increases the plausibility that a substantial portion of stock price movements may be due to noise created by irrational social pressures. The problem with this interesting approach is that Shiller provides no way to separate fads and pressures that do have effects on stock prices from those that do not. There is another approach that makes noise trading a permanent feature of the market which we can call *pervasive noise trader theory*.

Of primary importance is the fact that there are a great many financial firms (brokerage houses and investment advisors) whose income and existence depend on the belief that they have superior information than that provided by the investor himself or than that provided by prices themselves. They have managed to convince a great many investors that this is the case, and their continued existence is the best evidence of this. Pervasive noise trader theory recognizes that the institutional environment, the psychology of investors, and the economic incentives of stock sellers combine to provide powerful incentives to continue to produce a great deal of complex noise as a permanent feature of the stock market environment.

First, EMT is not simplistic and to understand it requires a firm grounding in neoclassical economic theory and statistical reasoning, a grounding that may change how one understands the way the economic world functions. Furthermore, to believe it strongly enough that one would guide one's behaviour by it requires an emotional commitment to using it. Only by time, effort and persuasion can one acquire the cognitive knowledge and the affective involvement with EMT to be able to give up the idea that one cannot consistently separate noise from information. The academic world does not do this very effectively in competing with alternative views of the world promulgated by investment advisors using sophisticated marketing techniques. Few investors outside the academy are likely to commit themselves to using EMT unless the investment world finds a reason to support it. Fortunately, Wall Street has learned that EMT can produce profits through the use of index funds based on EMT which have grown rapidly in recent years, holding over a half billion dollars in the USA. Nonetheless, Wall Street makes more money in the aggregate by producing a preponderance of noise over information and promoting an attitude of false hope and active investing behaviour, neither of which are implied by a belief in EMT.

For masculine investors, who dominate investing, the commitment goes deeper for this also means giving up their instinct for 'the hunt'. Consequently, investment advisors have been successful in debunking EMT to the average investor and playing on his belief that if he chooses the right hunting ground (a particular investing area such as technology or international or emerging market stocks) and selects a good weapon (stock advisor), and uses the proper hunting technique (acquires the good information) which others do not have the good fortune or skill to use, then he can bag the trophy (high-performance stock) and achieve status as the great hunter (shrewd stock picker). The often-heard complaint that random stock-picking strategies and mutual fund investing and dollar-cost averaging are not 'fun' suggests a strong psychological need for 'the hunt'. In consequence, security sellers constantly circulate stories about stocks, creating a permanent noise environment that in fact makes it possible, but not very probable, to bag those trophy stocks.

Second, stock advisors are rewarded for selling stocks in such a way that their interests are not very compatible with those they advise, a conflict called the *principal–agent problem*. One historic principal–agent problem is 'churning', the practice of rolling over a stock portfolio to gain fees. It is illegal but not uncommon, and with it a broker can make almost as much money when stocks go down as when they go up. Certainly, stockbrokers can make more in either case than if the shareholder uses a buy-and-hold strategy. Moreover, the problem is not confined to individual stock investing. A plethora of practices such as differential front-end loads, back-end loads, rolling loads, front-end and trailing commissions on 'no-load' funds and other fees all create principal–agent problems in the mutual fund field as well. Another aspect of this problem is that stock sellers receive differential commissions on different stock products, and this biases them to offer stock products for which they receive higher commissions rather than ones for which the buyers can make the highest risk-adjusted returns.

The low reputation of stockbrokers as a group compared with other economically comparable groups has a strong foundation. This could change if incentive structures in security advisor institutions are reformed, moving further toward fixed-fee incentives or, better still, performance fees wherein an advisor gains and loses money as the client does. A primary effect of this principal–agent problem is that it generates too much noise in the stock market, promoting too many stock transactions. This produces disequilibrium stock prices and greater stock price volatility.

Noise production will never be eliminated as long as people want actively managed stocks because information-only trading implies less trading and supports a much smaller investment-advising industry. Nonetheless, it could be seriously reduced. The pervasive noise trader theory implies that the only way seriously to reduce market noise is for the institutional and individual incentive environments to change so as to discourage noise production. Such changes would include a societal commitment to engaging potential investors more actively and earlier in the public educational system. Public education focuses on logic and evidence, and this would partially counter the persuasion by the investment world which is strongly biased by its economic incentive structure. Public knowledge of this could eventually result in the revamping of the set of economic incentives that guides information providers in the investment world to correlate more closely to those they advise. Fee-based accounts and, more powerfully, fees matching investors to advisor's performance would go a long way toward providing a lower noise/information ratio in the market and improving the tawdry image of the brokerage business. Also, as women become more involved in the market, it should become less irrational and more businesslike as human behaviour takes on less the character of a ritual hunt and more the character of a family farm. Historically, that has represented progress.

K.C.T.

REFERENCES

The Economist (1993), 'A Survey of the Frontiers of Finance' (9 October).
Fama, Eugene (1976), *Foundations of Finance*, New York: Basic Books.
Kolb, Robert W. (1992), *Investments*, 3rd edn, Miami, Florida: Kolb Publishing Company.
Shiller, Robert J. (1981), 'Stock Prices Move Too Much to be Justified by

Subsequent Changes in Dividends', *American Economic Review*, **71**, June, 421–36.

Shiller, Robert J. (1993), 'Stock Prices and Social Dynamics.' in Richard H. Thaler (ed.), *Advances in Behavioral Finance*, New York: Russell Sage Foundation, pp. 167–217. From *The Brookings Papers on Economic Activity* (1984), **71**, 457–510.

Thaler, Richard H. (1992), *The Winner's Curse: Paradoxes and Anomalies of Economic Life*, New York: Free Press.

24. The starvation of Buridan's ass

A hungry donkey faces two equally attractive stacks of hay. He is simply unable to decide which hay stack to go to. As a result, he starves. What's wrong with this case of indifference?

The fable of Buridan's ass was allegedly first told by Jean Buridan (c. 1295–1356), a Scholastic professor who taught, along with William of Ockham, at the University of Paris. The example of Buridan's ass was first used by theorists to justify the use of indifference curves in economic analysis (Schumpeter, 1954: 94, 1064).

According to the tale, the unfortunate animal starved to death because it was so placed midway between two equal bales of hay that it could not rationally choose between the two. Any argument it could find in favour of moving toward one bale was exactly offset by an equivalent argument in favour of moving toward the other. In short, the ass was totally 'indifferent', and therefore could not act.

Schumpeter (1954: 94n) refers to this ass as 'perfectly rational', but, in fact, there is no animal that could be less rational. From a logical point of view, there are actually three choices, the third being to starve where he is. Clearly, this third choice of starvation will be ranked lower in the donkey's revealed preferences than the other two on the donkey's value scale.

If both left and right bales of hay are equally preferable, the donkey will allow pure chance to decide on either one. No doubt it will not take the ass long to decide. It is absurd to deny the animal sufficient reason to choose at random (Rothbard, 1962: 267–8).

Ken Binmore has correctly assessed the logic of Buridan's burden:

> Buridan's conclusion is absurd, but not because his argument involves any logical fallacy. If one denies the ass access to any device that might be used to break the symmetry, like tossing a coin or consulting an ouija board, then it does indeed seem to follow that the ass will starve. The conclusion is fantastic because the hypothesis is fantastic. . . . (Binmore, 1994: 208)

M.S.

REFERENCES

Binmore, Ken (1994), *Playing Fair: Game Theory and the Social Contract*, **1**, Cambridge, Massachusetts: MIT Press.

Rothbard, Murray N. (1962), *Man, Economy and State*, Los Angeles, California: Nash Publishing.

Schumpeter, Joseph A. (1954), *History of Economic Analysis*, New York: Oxford University Press.

25. Does studying economics make one immoral?

Mainstream economic models are built upon the assumption that economic agents are economically rational. This behaviour is presumed to lead to societal well-being. However, many have argued that the adoption of this approach to understanding human behaviour creates a deep scepticism or even cynicism about human nature, leaving no room for belief in spontaneity, spirituality and altruism as important parts of the human character. Furthermore, it promotes the adoption of this behaviour even when it is not socially beneficent. If so, an approach that is justified by its beneficent social consequences ends up producing morally inferior people. Can we resolve this dilemma?

The view that a society in which market economic values dominates tends to produce people with muted moral sensibilities has been offered since Adam Smith and was a major theme in a well-known recent book (Bellah et al., 1985). One way the issue can be addressed is by looking at the behaviour of those who use such models to see if they demonstrate less moral behaviour, defined in some way. First we need to examine the nature of the models economists employ.

Economists, like other social scientists, employ heuristic assumptions intended to further our knowledge about human behaviour. Heuristic assumptions are not literally true but prove useful for the goal intended – which is to explain and predict human behaviour. Economists employ a common set of heuristic values embedded in key ideas. One of the most important of these ideas is economic efficiency – the idea that activities in the market which benefit at least one person and harm no one imply greater societal material well-being. Efficiency assumes a set of values for hypothetical humans in a model. Economists deal with efficiency in two primary ways: as a reference point against which to compare real world behaviour of alternatives and as a goal to which policy actions should strive. In using efficiency as a goal, personal and heuristic values are logically connected. In using efficiency as a reference point, they are logically distinct. However, even in the latter case, the attention given to efficiency suggests that it is an important concept. It is easy to imagine that an economist who continually used a concept and its implied set of heuristic values would hold or come to hold some or all of these heuristic values as personal values. What are these heuristic values underlying the efficiency concept?

First and most important, rationality, individual materialism and egoism are positively valued in economic models, not because they are intrinsically valuable, but they are instrumentally valuable because they provide incentives that motivate individuals to improve the material well-being of society. By trying to enrich themselves individuals motivate the market process and the result is the invisible hand of social betterment or economic efficiency. Rational action refers to behaviour that is consistent over time. Materialism means that people prefer more goods and services to less, and they value the goods and services themselves, not the process of producing them. Egoism implies that pursuit of self-interest is a dominant motive, and that human values are all that matter. Other animals, plants, and non-living things are not intrinsically valuable and have value only if people's actions value them. Moreover, at the base of materially driven egoism a social system of well-defined and stable property rights is assumed. These enable materially driven behaviour to be effective in achieving individual ends, which brings about the socially desirable goal of material betterment for society. In effect this implies that the existing structure and distribution of well-defined property rights which undergirds individual choice and the income and wealth distribution resulting from it are assumed to be fair or just. Changes in property rights and income and wealth distribution resulting over time from market choices are also fair, but changes in property rights or income and wealth distribution made through the political system are viewed more sceptically because they are not generated through a competitive market process, do not directly involve individual choice and are thus less likely to promote efficiency.

Second, each person's dollar vote reflects the values that people place on goods and services at the margin of decision making. The existence of a voluntary trade implies that both parties expect to be better off after the trade than before it. Consequently, interference with the market is to be avoided unless there are *market failures* – situations in which voluntary trade does not lead to the invisible hand. If market failures do exist, these are correctable with adjustments to the market (i.e. changing costs or fixing property rights problems) that allow prices to better perform their function of reflecting people's values.

Third, each person's dollar vote counts equally regardless of any other characteristics the person has, including their income and wealth levels. If person A wants to spend $10 000 on a product as compared to the $10 from person B, person A has 1000 times more economic 'votes' than person B. 'Economic fairness' resides in the fact that each dollar registers equally with no other forms of discrimination valued in the efficiency concept.

Fourth, the more choices people have in the market the better off is society because individual preferences can be more completely reflected in market outcomes. Moreover, the resulting trades are more likely to produce greater net benefits for the parties involved. Both ideas imply greater economic efficiency.

Again, as a logical matter, economists need not adopt these heuristic values as personal moral values in order to use them in theories. The hypothetical humans in economic models who hold these values do not necessarily serve as models for those real humans doing the analysis. Yet psychologically it may be difficult for mainstream economists to clearly separate their personal values from heuristic values. This is certainly true of economists who utilize an understanding of human behaviour that sees some choices as better than others in terms of economic efficiency. Since the goal of economic efficiency is considered to be an important and useful idea which motivates a great deal of economic analysis, it invariably becomes suffused with a moral dimension. Otherwise, why would economists use it? Right behaviour is that which promotes economic efficiency, and if economic efficiency is valued positively by economists, the values of the hypothetical humans inhabiting economic models whose behaviour leads to economic efficiency likewise would tend to be positively valued. Frank, Gilovich and Regan (1996: 192) assert that ' . . . all parties concede that economics training encourages the view that people are primarily motivated by self interest'. Let's see what is implied if economists (including students of economics) personally adopt all the heuristic values of the economic agents in their models.

We would expect economists to value efficiency as a goal more than the general population. We would expect economists to believe that people are rational, egoistic and materialistic in their behaviour and consequently less spontaneous, altruistic and spiritual than the general population would believe. We would also expect economists to be more conservative with respect to the desirability of politically changing property rights to achieve economic goals. In addition, we would expect the following behaviours to be found in greater proportion among economists than the general population: the translation of a variety of values into the single metric of money, recommending solutions to society's problems that utilize the market process, stressing the equality of opportunity to choose rather than the equality of the outcomes of choice, and recommending solutions involving more choices, other things being equal. Notions that efficiency should be subordinated to non-economic goals, that egoistic and materialistic behaviour is immoral and could be responsible for a long-run decline in the standard of living, that monetary calculations are irrelevant or inappropriate for some societal problems, that community directed rather than individually directed solutions are needed to solve many problems, that too many choices overwhelm our ability to process information efficiently will tend to be rejected proportionately more by economists compared to the general population if the heuristic values noted are adopted as personal values.

Most of these propositions have not been studied at all, and only one has been systematically investigated empirically. With respect to materialistic rationality well-controlled auction market experiments have been extensively studied for more than 25 years (Smith, 1989). These auction market experimental games use actual cash to pay buyers and sellers to participate and reward them with more money for better market performance. There is strong evidence from these games in a variety of auction markets that, while students experienced in economics may initially play market experimental games more successfully, differential performance between experienced and non-experienced students disappears rather quickly in playing these games, and equilibrium is reached rapidly (Smith, 1982: 170). The conclusion from these experiments is that rational materially driven self-interest promotes equilibrium and efficiency even more strongly than the neoclassical model assumes. However, auction markets do not involve social dilemmas, and it is these that make individual rational behaviour socially irrational.

This kind of research has begun to be developed by economists. They have been asking whether or not the study of economics tends to produce more egocentric, less cooperative behaviour (Frank, Gilovich and Regan, 1993) in situations where it is not beneficent to society – social dilemmas. Most of the studies that have been done have looked at whether or not economists, including economics students, tend to be more egoistically rational and therefore less cooperative, less altruistic, and less charitable than people who are not students of economics. Most of these studies have taken the form of surveys or games that are played without experimental controls, rather than being based on field observations or well-controlled experimentation. As a result alternative hypotheses from the ones supported by this research are plausible. The conclusions, as the authors note, are merely suggestive, not definitive. To what conclusions do they come?

One conclusion from gaming situations was that students of economics were less altruistic (Marwell and Ames, 1981; Carter and Irons,

1991; Frank, Gilovich and Regan, 1993) and had less belief that this quality involved fairness (Marwell and Ames, 1981) than students not in economics. Another conclusion based on survey data was that professional economists tended to give, adjusted for income level, about 10 per cent less to charities and more of them gave nothing as compared to other social and natural scientists surveyed. Another gaming situation with a follow-up survey concluded that the lower level of cooperation revealed by economics majors compared to non-economics majors seemed to be due to the training they received in mainstream economics and not to the self-selection of students who choose to major in economics because they are just naturally more rationally egoistic (Frank, Gilovich and Regan, 1993). Another result based on a survey of economics students with two different types of course (Frank, Gilovich and Regan, 1993) concluded that training in conventional economics makes students less honest – or more cynical. However, when Yezar, Goldfarb and Poppen (1996) duplicated this survey, they did not find any statistically significant difference between students exposed to and not exposed to conventional economics in terms of honesty. Moreover, in a letter-drop experiment in which actual behaviour was studied these researchers found evidence that economics students were more honest than non-economics students.

What can we conclude from this research? Unfortunately, very little. There is weak evidence that economists are less cooperative in social dilemma situations than non-economists. If such research becomes better supported, a case for the greater immorality of economists than non-economists could be made. Even if we accept this conclusion, it is not clear that the study of economics is responsible for much if any of the immorality. This less cooperative behaviour could be an acquired 'moral' value due to the training that economists undertake in successfully using the heuristic values in the typical models discussed to understand reality. But it is also plausible that economists are attracted to the discipline because they already hold these heuristic values as moral values to a greater extent than the general population. In either case, why should we expect economists to be *more* honest than others, as the letter-drop experiment suggested? Even less is known about the other behaviours implied by adoption of the heuristic values of mainstream economics since no studies have examined these. Does studying economics make one immoral? Speculation is all we have for now. This remains a fascinating and rich area for empirical research for psychologists and economists.

K.C.T.

REFERENCES

Bellah, Robert N. et al. (1985), *Habits of the Heart: Individualism and Commitment in American Life*, Berkeley, California: University of California Press.

Carter, John and Michael Irons (1991), 'Are Economists Different, and If So, Why?' *Journal of Economic Perspectives*, **5** (2), 171–7.

Frank, Robert H., Thomas D. Gilovich and Dennis T. Regan (1993), 'Does Studying Economics Inhibit Cooperation?' *Journal of Economic Perspectives*, **7** (2) 159–71.

Frank, Robert H., Thomas D. Gilovich and Dennis T. Regan (1996), 'Do Economists Make Bad Citizens?' *Journal of Economic Perspectives*, **10** (1), 187–92.

Marwell, Gerald and Ruth Ames (1981), 'Economists Free Ride, Does Anyone Else?: Experiments on the Provision of Public Goods, IV', *Journal of Public Economics*, **15** (3), 295–310.

Smith, Vernon (1982), 'Markets as Economizers of Information: Experimental Examination of the "Hayek Hypothesis"', *Economic Inquiry*, **20** (2), 165–79.

Smith, Vernon (1989), 'Theory, Experiment and Economics', *Journal of Economic Perspectives*, (3) 1, 151–69.

Yezar, Anthony M., Robert S. Goldfarb and Paul J. Poppen, (1996), 'Does Studying Economics Discourage Cooperation? Watch What We Do, Not What We Say or How We Play', *Journal of Economic Perspectives*, **10** (1), 177–86.

26. The savers' dilemma

The public's desire to increase the saving rate expands the supply of saving, which reduces the interest rate paid on savings accounts. As a result, people are discouraged from saving and decide to save less. Therefore, it is impossible to change the saving rate. Correct?

Not so fast. Standard supply and demand analysis can resolve this problem; see Figure 26.1. As the figure demonstrates, the initial effect of increased saving by the public is to shift S to S'. The total amount of saving expands from A to B. But at point B, the banks do not need to pay the current rate to attract more savings. Excessive saving permits the banks to lower interest rates on their passbook saving accounts and certificates of deposit. It is true that this decline in the rate discourages

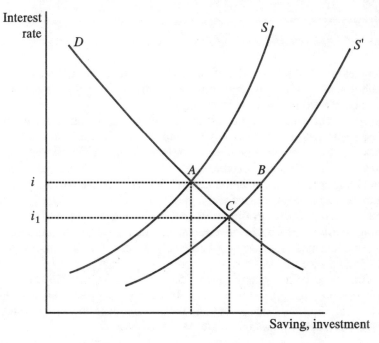

Figure 26.1   Supply and demand for savings

127

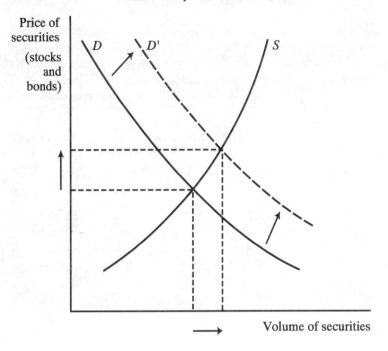

Figure 26.2   Supply and demand for securities

some investors, but not all. The final point of equilibrium is *C*, somewhere between *A* and *B*. In short, the secondary decline in savings does not exceed the initial increase in savings.

Moreover, the decline in interest rates itself increases other forms of savings, i.e. stocks and bonds. When interest rates decline, stocks and bonds look more attractive compared to bank savings accounts and certificates of deposit. Some of the money moves out of bank savings accounts and into stocks and bonds. The dissaving at the banks results in an increase in investment in securities.

Figure 26.2 demonstrates the effect of lower interest rates in the stock and bond markets. Here a lower interest rate increases the demand and supply of securities (stocks and bonds). The result is higher prices for securities and more new issues.

In sum, the increased desire to save does effectively increase savings, despite the pressure on interest rates. In turn the lower interest rate induces other kinds of saving so that the net increase in saving could be greater than the initial aggregate desire to save.

M.S.

27. Keynes's banana plantation

What would happen if a community that only produces bananas decides to save more? The same number of bananas is produced, but people spend less money on bananas. Prices fall, profits turn to losses, workers are laid off, income drops, and even fewer bananas are sold. Eventually, the community starves to death. How can you resolve Keynes's dilemma?

In *A Treatise on Money*, published in 1930, the British economist John Maynard Keynes (1883–1946) raised the prospect that savings could be 'abortive' if not invested. Keynes pointed out that in today's world, saving is different from investing. Saving is a 'negative act of refraining from spending', while investment is a 'positive act of starting or maintaining some process of production'. Hence, savings and investment could grow apart, creating a business cycle (Keynes, 1971 [1930]: 155).

Keynes used an analogy of a banana plantation to demonstrate his point. Suppose a community devotes its entire production to bananas and members of the community engage in a thrift campaign at a time when the plantation needs no additional investment capital. The same number of bananas is produced, but because of lower final demand, the price of bananas falls. The total crop is sold, but the banana producers suffer a loss. Costs of production remain the same, but total revenues have fallen. The plantation owners are therefore forced to reduce wages or lay off workers, either of which causes a reduction in the spending power of the public. In turn, consumers buy even less bananas, which results in more layoffs. This vicious cycle continues until there is no banana production at all and the community starves to death. The only solution is to call off the thrift campaign (Keynes, 1971 [1930]: 158–60).

Keynes's savings dilemma is resolved by going back to his assumptions about the banana plantation. He assumes that the community is distinct from the plantation business. The community desires its members to save more, while the plantation owners have no need for capital improvements. Yet if the only business in the community is banana production, the community *is* the banana company, and there would be no separation between saving and investing. Typically, people don't save without a goal in mind. If the community desired more saving, it would be to fulfil a specific need – perhaps to invest in new machinery, tools, or technology that will reduce costs, increase market share, and expand profitability of the banana factory. Or for retirement, future consumption, etc.

Also, Keynes ignores the role of interest rates in his example. A new thrift campaign would increase the supply of capital and reduce interest rates. In turn, the cost of leasing machinery and tools in the production of bananas would fall, thus allowing the profit *margins* to stay the same. Prices of bananas have fallen (due to reduced consumer demand), but the cost of production has also fallen. Therefore, the company will not have to lay off workers.

M.S.

REFERENCES

Keynes, John Maynard (1971 [1930]), *A Treatise on Money*, London: Macmillan.
Skousen, Mark (1992), 'Keynes and the Anti-Saving Mentality', in Mark Skousen (ed.), *Dissent on Keynes: A Critical Appraisal of Keynesian Economics*, New York: Praeger.

28. Producing cars that don't sell

In a Forbes *column (6 August 1990), economist Alan Reynolds asks,* *'Does it make sense for people to buy fewer cars so that manufacturers can build more auto factories?' How do you respond to this criticism of savings?*

Normally, an expanding economy involves an increase in savings, consumption and production simultaneously. If business is more profitable, wages and salaries increase and people have more income. Higher income is typically divided into more saving and more spending. Hence consumers might buy more cars while at the same time putting more money away in bank savings or brokerage accounts.

But what if incomes are flat, expectations are pessimistic, and people decide to save more by cutting back on consumer expenditures such as automobiles? Obviously, the demand for new automobiles falls, and inventories rise on dealers' lots. Automobile manufacturers in Detroit and elsewhere consider cutting back on production.

At the same time, a higher saving rate means an increase in the supply of savings, which can be used for business expansion. But why would automobile manufacturers consider expanding their auto production in the face of falling consumer demand and pessimistic expectations? This is Alan Reynolds's query. Actually, the answer could be affirmative. Here's how: suppose the increased supply of savings reduces long-term interest rates. Lower interest rates mean that the auto dealers can offer cheaper consumer loans, thus reducing the overall cost of automobile ownership. Car buyers can afford to buy the same number of cars, even though they are now saving. Lower interest rates could reverse consumer pessimism.

In addition, lower interest rates may encourage automobile manufacturers to increase capital investment – spending more on retooling, upgrading or building new plants, and developing new, better models.

We must not ignore the time factor. People spend less now in order to increase their consumer spending later. Sometime in the future, consumers will take those savings (which have earned interest, dividends and capital gains) and spend them on consumption goods. By then the auto manufacturers may have higher-quality cars available for purchase.

To demonstrate the positive possibilities in Alan Reynolds's case, consider the story of Henry Ford's Model A. In the late 1920s, new marketing and technical challenges forced the Ford Motor Company to shut down and revamp its entire plant in Detroit. Due to increased competition by General Motors and Chrysler, the famous Model T had become obsolete, falling way behind in sales. GM and other auto manufacturers offered a wider variety of styles and colour. (Ford was initially stubborn when it came to colour changes. He said, 'You can have any colour you want as long as it's black'.) By May 1927, Ford had stopped output altogether, shutting down production for nearly a year to devote all its efforts toward redesigning a new, improved Model A. Sixty thousand workers were temporarily laid off. Salesmen quit and worked for competitors. Ford customers bought GM cars. Investors waited, and there was pessimism in the air. Meanwhile, Ford spent $100 million developing the new model which, once designed, required the redesigning and creation of thousands of new machine tools, dies and fixtures. It was a gigantic capital undertaking. But the wait was worthwhile. The Model A proved to be extremely popular when it appeared in late 1928 (Skousen, 1990: 225). As historian Jonathan Hughes states, 'By 1933 Ford sold fewer cars than either General Motors or Chrysler, but the bottom had been reached and there was no danger of extinction. In a mere six years, from Model T to V8, Ford had caught up and surpassed, technically, his competitors in many respects' (Hughes, 1986: 336).

Where did Ford get $100 million to revamp his factory? From earnings the company had retained over the years when Ford was profitable.

Although the Ford Model A story is an example of a dynamic 'micro' model, it could apply to a case of 'macro'. Suppose consumers turn pessimistic about the future and temporarily stop buying retail goods – cars, appliances, clothing, computers, etc. Inventories build up and workers are laid off. But there is a silver lining to the cloud – interest rates fall, and companies offer special discounts and cheap loans. Lower financing and lower prices encourage consumers. Lower interest rates also reduce the costs of capital formation and encourage new business opportunities. As a result, the wave of pessimism is abated.

M.S.

REFERENCES

Hughes, Jonathan (1986), *The Vital Few*, New York: Oxford University Press.
Reynolds, Alan (1990), 'Masochistic Statistics', *Forbes*, **146** (3), 129.
Skousen, Mark (1990), *The Structure of Production*, New York: New York University Press.

29. The feckless forecast and policy purveyor puzzle

'GDP will grow by 1–2 per cent next year and inflation will be in the 3–4 per cent range.' This kind of forecast is continually being made by business economists. 'To regain our eroding living standards we must become more internationally competitive.' Such policy pronouncements are regularly made in the media by economists. Yet such forecasts are frequently wrong, and these policy statements are frequently misguided. They both often overstate the extent of knowledge we have about the economy. This undermines the credibility of economics and economic analysis. Yet it persists. Why?

The problem of experts claiming to know more than they do is not unique to economics. It is also a problem in the field of medicine, where Dr Suzanne Fletcher, in referring to disease prevention and health measures says, 'we tend to communicate more certainty than we have' (Kolata, 1995: B7). Why would experts put their own and their profession's credibility on the line when making more modest claims is both more accurate and less risky professionally? The answer lies in the alternative sets of values that motivate academic research and other endeavours, and the different incentive structure this implies. Economic analysis can help us understand this.

Mainstream economics is built on simple assumptions about human behaviour. Most fundamentally, it assumes that in general people are rational. At the very least this means that people are consistent in making choices. When economic analysis is applied to economic market processes, humans are also assumed to be materially driven and self-interested. Economists recognize that these three assumptions do not apply to everyone, nor to anyone all of the time. But in the context of exchange that is motivated by non-egoistic or non-material interests, it will usually be material concerns (price, quality, quantity, one's income) that will dominate the particular choice made in the exchange. So long as material self-interest motivates people at the time of the exchange decision, these become the relevant variables in understanding behaviour.

We can think of higher educational institutions as markets in the sense that exchanges take place and scarce resources are expended. Academic market values are, in general, different from and in some ways antithetical to economic market values. The primary mission of colleges and universities is the search for knowledge and wisdom and encouraging others to share in that goal both for their own edification, and because they can improve their material living standards. A number of shared values derive from this mission.

The value most relevant to understanding the puzzle is the desire of academics to understand physical and behavioural processes with intellectually rigorous reasoning, commonly called critical thinking. Intellectual rigour implies thinking through the logic of an argument or approach wherever it leads, questioning assumptions, and confronting a theoretical argument with evidence. The main reward for academics is the respect and prestige they have among their colleagues; the salary that they earn or the public recognition they achieve are clearly secondary rewards. Research institutions are the most prestigious venues for an academic career, and the primary way a professor gains respect and admiration is from the quantity and quality of research based on intellectual rigour. Neither a six-figure salary nor recognition by a wider public earn one the influence and respect available from one's colleagues. Indeed, if these rewards are accompanied by erroneous predictions and incorrect diagnoses of societal problems they earn the opprobrium of academics. Why then do we constantly read and hear erroneous economic forecasts and ill-considered policy pronouncements by economic experts? The answer is that there are other markets with different values that some economists choose to participate in instead of or in addition to the academic market.

One such market is the business market. Here the major goal of firms is, of course, to make substantial or maximum profits. Within this market there is a submarket for economic advice to the firm, either from economists employed by the firm or contracted from an economic advice organization. Business economists who work for firms are like other employees in that their shared values are those of the firm, which are to make substantial or maximum profits. The same is true of business economists who run their own firm. To be sure, business economists have professional values, notably intellectual rigour, but this is subordinated to the overarching profit-making goal of the firm. This means that business economists need to develop models that are of interest to the firm and must come up with answers to firms' policy questions in terms of macroeconomics (what is the direction of long-term interest rates and Fed policy for the next year?) and microeconomics (if we raise our price 10 per cent, will our total revenue increase?). A strong corporate value is placed on answers to these questions, and business economists who develop a reputation for good answers communicated clearly and with authority command higher salaries and prestige within the business world, the primary vocational community of business economists. A legitimate uncertainty driven by the value of intellectual rigour has far less credibility than it does in academia, not only because the technical nature of the models is difficult to communicate to the primary audience who are non-economist managers, but also because there is a significant demand for answers that one can have confidence in for planning business activities. Consequently, there is a strong tendency to produce answers to business questions even when the business economist has a tenuous basis for them. The result turns out to be a regular proliferation of forecasts, many not borne out by reality. In fact these forecasts tend to be cautious as most business forecasts of key economic variables such as interest rates and bond yields tend to be extrapolations from recent data. Trends develop and often continue and such predictions turn out to be reasonably accurate.

However, it is the dramatic changes that business firms most want to know about, for these are most likely to alter their profit picture substantially. Yet these dramatic changes in trend are most likely to be missed by business forecasters. Fifty business economists' average prediction of long-term bond yields was that they would finish 1995 at 7.86 per cent, a figure very close to the rate when the predictions were made. In fact, a substantial bond rally sent yields down to 6 per cent (Lowenstein, 1995). These erroneous predictions did not hurt a particular business economist who badly missed calling bond yields as much as one might think, since most business economists at other firms also missed badly. Expectations of performance are shaped by the standards of the community one is in. An economic forecaster can make plenty of mistakes and still be considered an average or a prescient forecaster if most others are making similar or more mistakes, respectively. In any case, one cannot choose not to make predictions if the goals of the firm call for them and one's peers are doing so. Consequently, the proliferation of wrong forecasts, especially at the most critical times, will continue.

Another market is the political market. Politicians are motivated by the desire for political power and the public prestige that comes with it. They may have a variety of other motivations including the desire to do good, to improve the competence of politics, to promote a set of values, or even to make a high income through political connections. But the motivation that politicians share is the desire to acquire and retain political power, for without these, the other motivations are unlikely to be achieved. Within this overarching market for political power there exists a submarket for advice to politicians. There is a strong and persistent political advice market for answers to economic questions and solutions to economic problems that rewards the providers of these answers and solutions with money and power. This is true because the state of the economy and the expectations of the economic future often determine elections. Politicians must deal with multiple constituencies and with a myriad of issues, some of them conflicting and virtually all of them requiring tradeoffs. The benefits to some constituencies associated with a proposed policy change will be costs to other constituencies. If benefits are diffuse (such as lower prices to consumers) and costs are concentrated (such as the removal of subsidies from a group of sellers), the proposed policy change will be a political dead end because the intensity of preferences of the sellers is stronger than that of the consumers even though consumers vastly outnumber sellers. This would be reflected in the time, energy and money that the sellers are willing to devote to the election of their candidate as compared to consumers. Consequently, politicians are always on the lookout for experts who can provide simple, interesting and easily communicated policy options that reduce or eliminate these conflicts. They, or their aides, often have a rudimentary understanding of these conflicts and a sense of some possible solutions to them, but they do not have the substantive knowledge that would allow them to create a story or vision that they can communicate to the public to gain or enhance their political power. Often these are not available from the academic community.

Academic research economists place the highest value on working out the substantive nature of problems and potential solutions to them within an intellectually rigorous framework. In economics this means the use of formal economic models built on specific and necessarily restrictive assumptions to identify principles and relationships to help explain reality. These models are often difficult to translate into policy prescriptions because the model assumptions do not hold exactly in reality, and policy options that are presented must include both the size and distribution of gains and losses associated with the proposed policy to have academic credibility. Academics then often tend to be cautious about drawing conclusions about the real world from these models. Moreover, conclusions that are drawn often tend not to give dramatic net benefits once total costs and benefits are accounted for, and even policies that do are carefully circumscribed because of the quantitative uncertainty surrounding estimates of economic effects. In a curious similarity to politicians, economists also prefer simple, clear-cut solutions to economic problems. But they have only found these – and only rarely too – in economic *theory* under specified assumptions. For this reason, among academic economists policy matters take a back seat to economic theorizing which, in keeping with the values noted, has the highest prestige in the academic community.

Nonetheless, since searching for simple solutions is a shared methodological value, and a strong political market beckons for those economists who can explain and communicate economic ideas with clear-cut policy conclusions, political rewards can be reaped by those economists who become what Paul Krugman (1994: 10–15) calls *policy entrepreneurs*. Not all policy entrepreneurs are academic economists, but those who are almost invariably trade off influence and prestige within the economics profession for power and influence (and impressive speaking fees) with politicians and the general public. Policy entrepreneurs such as Arthur Laffer and Robert Reich speak and write articulately about economic ideas and issues, conveying an understandable story to those untrained in economics and purveying policies that are sharply defined with clear-cut benefits and few if any costs, values unappreciated by those whose primary value is theoretical rigour but greatly appreciated by the general public who do not hold these values very strongly, if at all. Such policies are not taken seriously by academic economists because they invariably look for tradeoffs lurking in the background of any policy change. Politicians do not like to discuss tradeoffs because that means alienating some constituency; consequently, they or their aides are always on the lookout for articulate policy entrepreneurs who can tell 'win–win' stories in which gains to some people are not accompanied by losses to anyone else. Krugman presents as exemplars of publicly attractive but theoretically flawed macroeconomic policies, the supply-side story by conservatives in the 1980s (1994: 82–103) and the strategic trader policies of neoliberals in the 1990s (1994: 245–67). Such views never had much influence or prestige in the academic community because they omitted important theoretical principles, distorted others, ignored salient facts and did not address costs that conflicted with the story they were telling. In short, they lacked intellectual rigour. However, the general public found them to be credible and attractive stories. In both cases there were many academically high-powered conservative and liberal academic economists respectively who eschewed the supply-side policies and strategic trade policies being promoted in the media, but had no simple and easily communicable alternative set of policies they could confidently offer.

Academic economists do advocate economic policy and do so persuasively. John Maynard Keynes was the most prominent example in this century. More recently, different policies based on alternative views about the way modern economies function have been put forth to the general public by famous economists. In the 1960s and 1970s Milton Friedman (1912–) and Paul Samuelson (1915–), both Nobel laureates, offered regular economic policy advice for government and public consumption based on monetarist and neo-Keynesian perspectives respectively. Their policy prescriptions were credible to economists because they were based on theoretically rigorous (though quite distinct) economic theories, and, it must be said, because of the prestige they had accumulated as academic economists. When reality had rendered both of these visions suspect by the late 1970s, mainstream economics evolved the new contending visions represented by new classical, new Keynesian, and real business cycle theories.

In conclusion, economists often overstate the extent of knowledge we have about the economy because there are multiple markets for economic ideas, and different values associated with them. The values of academic economists are most at variance with those of business economists and policy entrepreneurs, but consistent with the market in which they participate. Both business economists and policy entrepreneurs are driven by a more market-like set of values in the sense that materialism is a driving force for their behaviour. The desire of the firm for profits shapes the behaviour of the business economist, and the desire of the politician for political power shapes the behaviour of policy entrepreneurs. While the academic value of theoretical rigour that attracted many of them to economic graduate programmes also influences their behaviour, it becomes much less important than it is for academic economists. Theoretical rigour negates the impulse to present and promote questionable economic policy solutions where these cannot be justified by theory and evidence, fully and carefully considered. There is no political or business market for uncertainty about problems and solutions because this yields no political power or profits to the politician or firm. Obviously, the more education business leaders, their stockholders, and the public have about the nature of economic reality, the less willing they will be to believe exaggerated theories and unsubstantiated claims from corporate heads and politicians, and the smaller the market will be for forecasting business economists and policy entrepreneurs. This also suggests the importance of the maintenance of academic values, where the truth of an idea and willingness to state one's lack of certainty is more valued than the expectations of profit, high salaries, or the political power one can obtain by providing well-communicated answers with an untruthful certainty.

K.C.T.

REFERENCES

Kolata, Gina (1995), 'Amid Inconclusive Health Studies, Some Experts Advise Less Advice', *New York Times*, 10 May, B7.
Krugman, Paul (1994), *Peddling Prosperity*, New York: W.W. Norton.
Lowenstein, Roger (1995), 'For Market Seers, Vision Is Best in Hindsight', *Wall Street Journal*, 28 December, C1.

30. The growing but declining gap puzzle

The income gap between rich and poor countries is growing at the same time that poor countries are gaining on the rich. How can this be so? What does this mean for the future of the poor?

The income gap question has been important since the 1960s (Ward, Runnels and D'Anjou, 1971). The easier but often confused part of the issue finds resolution by examination of the quantitative implications of distinguishing between changes in levels of income and differences in rates of change in income among countries over time. But once we make this distinction, the second and more important question becomes difficult to address.

When numerical values differ a great deal, it is likely that even with a much higher growth rate for the lower value, the difference between the lower and higher value can become greater for a while before it begins to decline and ultimately exceeds the higher value. This is what has happened with the income gap between more developed and less developed countries. The most commonly used measure of economic well-being is per capita gross national product. Table 30.1 (World Bank, 1995: Table 1) shows per capita gross national product for different years given the low-income country growth rate of 3.7 per cent for the 1980–93 period, and the high-income country growth rate of 2.2 per cent for the same period. Using the present value of a stock formula we have future year = base year $(1+g)^t$ where g is the annual growth rate and t is the number of years of growth. Table 30.1 also shows the size of the income gap in 1980 and 1993, 2262 when it begins to close, and 2296 when it finally closes altogether.

From Table 30.1 we can see that the per capita GNP gap between low-income and high-income countries will grow for a long time before peaking and then declining. But we should hardly take these data seriously.

Per capita GNP does not grow at a constant rate as Table 30.1 assumes it does – even on the average for the group of low-income or high-income countries. For example, if we take the average annual per

141

Table 30.1   Growth gaps with alternative constant growth rates

	Per capita GNP, 1980	Per capita GNP, 1993	Per capita GNP, 2262	Per capita GNP, 2296
Low-income ave. annual growth rate of 3.7 per cent	$237	$280	$4 916 358	$16 909 128
High-income ave. annual growth rate of 2.2 per cent	$17 400	$23 090	$8 048 499	$16 867 292
Size of gap	$17 163	$22 810	$3 132 142	~0

capita GNP growth for the 1960–81 period (World Bank, 1983: Table 1), we see that low-income economies grew at 2.9 per cent while high-income economies grew at 3.4 per cent, a reversal of direction from the later period. Had we extrapolated these figures through the subsequent periods we would have drawn very different conclusions about the pattern of relative change since the gap would never close! We can see that changes in the measured growth rate can alter the perception of the nature of the problem over time. What earlier was a widening growth rate gap problem has more recently become the widening income gap problem despite the apparent reversal of growth rates for low-income and high-income countries. Of course, we could argue that the two periods 1960–81 and 1980–93 are not comparable since the number of countries designated as low-income changed significantly from 34 to 45 in the later period, although none in the earlier period made it to the middle-income group of countries. In fact concerns about country composition raise a more important issue about such group growth rate comparisons.

The data used represent average per capita GNP across two groups of countries. An average only represents the members of the group if the individual values cluster tightly around the average, like the familiar bell curve, being little dispersed and not skewed. Otherwise, generalizations from averages prove uninformative. But for low-income country comparisons such is the case. The per capita GNP average of $380 in 1993 is composed of individual country data which are very dispersed. The range of per capita GNP goes from $90 for Mozambique to $660 for Egypt for low-income countries while for high-income countries it is much less dispersed, going from $12 600 for New Zealand to $35 760 for Switzerland. Furthermore, the rate of growth of per capita GNP for country groupings is weighted by the size of GNP. Low-income country per capita GNP growth rate is highly skewed by the presence of two large countries, China and India, that had growth rates of 8.2 per cent and 3.0 per cent respectively for the 1980–93 period. When we take them out of the low-income country group, the average annual growth rate falls from 3.7 per cent to 0.1 per cent (for the 1960–81 period, the low-income growth rate falls from 2.9 per cent to 0.8 per cent). In fact of the 38 countries for which data were available in the 1980–93 period, 23 of them had negative growth rates over the period while only two of 24 high-income countries had negative growth rates. For high-income countries the greater weight from the high growth rate of Japan skews the rate of 2.2 per cent only slightly.

That is, once we disaggregate the data and look more specifically at the individual low-income country data, a very different picture of material progress for the group of low-income countries emerges than that implied by looking only at the averages. If our purpose is to understand what is happening in most low-income compared to most high-income countries, average annual per capita GNP comparisons for these groups of countries are virtually meaningless. If we are willing to extrapolate these data, a questionable exercise, we could conclude that most rich countries are getting richer and most poor countries are getting poorer in both absolute terms – the per capita GNP gap is widening – and in relative terms – the per capita GNP growth rate is lower for most low-income countries. The situation will get worse and worse over time! But each piece of data is itself an average of incomes within each country. How about the distribution and skewness of incomes within countries? How does income distribution differ among low-income and high-income countries?

Neither the level nor the growth rate of per capita GNP gives useful information about the proportion of rich and poor within a country. Income distribution data are scarce in low-income countries, and our primary information about income distribution for low-income countries has so far come from cross-section studies.

Simon Kuznets (1955), on the basis of the scanty evidence available at that time, suggested that as per capita GNP rises for a low-income country, income inequality increases, peaks at a middle-income level, and then declines as high income is reached. If we look at these three groups of countries with more recent data, the Kuznets hypothesis holds up well (Gillis et al., 1992: 84–5). The rich get richer and the poor get poorer for a while before the situation reverses.

However, a key problem with these cross-section data is that they measure differences across countries over time, not changes in income distribution within a country over time – as do time series data. Time series data are what we really want in order to determine what happens to the proportion of rich and poor within a country over time. Cross-section data can serve as a proxy for time series data only if cross-section differences among countries mirror time series changes within a country over time. That is, we must assume that a common qualitative and quantitative pattern to economic development applies to all countries. If countries go through the same pattern of development, then as per capita GNP increases across low-income countries, income distribution should become more unequal. This is a strong and dubious assumption given what we can observe about differences in income distribution for low-income countries for which data are available (World Bank, 1995: Table 30). The limited amount of time series evidence available does not permit us to draw a conclusion about the Kuznets hypothesis. The resolution of the Kuznets hypothesis will have to await future time series data for income distribution in individual countries. If the Kuznets hypothesis is borne out, this will mean that as material well-being, as measured by per capita GNP, increases for low-income countries, the situation for the poorest within each country will get worse before it gets better.

K.C.T.

REFERENCES

Gillis, Malcolm, Dwight H. Perkins, Michael Roemer and Donald R. Snodgrass (1992), *Economics of Development*, 3rd edn, New York: W.W. Norton.
Kuznets, Simon (1995), 'Economic Growth and Income Inequality', *American Economic Review*, **45** (1), March.
Ward, Barbara, J.D. Runnels and Lenore D'Anjou (1971), *The Widening Gap – Development in the 1970s*, New York: Columbia University Press.
World Bank (1983; 1995), *World Development Reports 1983; 1995*, New York: Oxford University Press.

31. The perpetual poverty puzzle

In his 1964 State of the Union address President Lyndon Johnson declared a 'War on Poverty' to eliminate poverty in the USA and create economic self-sufficiency. Since then the federal government has devoted billions of dollars to doing so. The policy has failed and poverty, by some measures, has actually become worse over the past 20 years. Why cannot the wealthiest country in world history put an end to poverty, or even reduce it significantly?

Poverty can be understood in absolute or relative terms. *Absolute poverty* results when a family falls below a socially defined threshold of goods and services, usually measured by income. In principle, absolute poverty can be eliminated if all families have more than the threshold level of income. *Relative poverty* exists for families below a socially determined threshold percentage of income for the whole society, say families in the lowest 10 per cent of the population in terms of income. Relative poverty is perpetual and can never be eliminated since a lowest given percentage of the population in terms of income must always exist. However, when President Johnson made the 'War on Poverty' statement, he had an absolute conception of poverty in mind of which there already existed a measure.

Mollie Orshansky of the Social Security Administration developed a conceptually simple absolute definition of poverty based on spending patterns of US families in 1955. Surveys showed that about one-third of all expenditures of a typical family went toward food. Classifying families by size and composition, male/female head, and farm/non-farm classifications, Orshansky developed minimal food budgets for each of the possible patterns and then multiplied these by three to obtain the poverty income threshold for various family types. The Bureau of the Budget made the *poverty rate* – the percentage of households or families below the poverty threshold – the basis for the official government measure of poverty in 1969, and this is still in use today with some modifications. The official poverty threshold is compared with before-tax income including social security and social insurance plus means-tested government cash transfers: aid to families with dependent children, non-federal public assistance, supplemental security income, and veterans' payments. The official poverty measure excludes means-tested non-cash transfers: food stamps, school lunches, Medicaid, and rent subsidies. The poverty thresholds rise each year according to the consumer price index (CPI). In 1964 the average poverty threshold for a family of four was $3169 and by 1992 it was $14 335 (US Department of Commerce, 1992: A-6).

At a macroeconomic level the solution to poverty seems transparent. Absolute poverty can be reduced or eliminated in three ways: by the economic system generating real income growth since a general rise in real income will eventually move families above the poverty threshold; by government policy which redistributes some of the non-poverty incomes to those in poverty; and by government creation of new programmes targeted to help those in poverty overcome it. President Johnson and his advisors evidently believed that real economic growth, the progressivity of the federal tax system, appropriately directed government expenditures, and new government programmes could be combined to eliminate poverty within a decade.

The War on Poverty did not succeed. If we look at Table 31.1, column A shows that the official poverty rate fell from 1964 to 1974 by about 41 per cent, only to rise after that so that the 1993 poverty rate was only 21 per cent less than the 1964 rate. In addition, column B shows that the number of people in poverty in 1993 was higher than in 1964. Moreover, aggregate figures conceal great variation among states and in their experience over time. From 1980 to 1990 the poverty rate went up in 30 states and down in 22 states, and in 1990 it varied from a high of 25.7 per cent in Mississippi to a low of 6.0 per cent in Connecticut (Kimenyi, 1995: 102–3). Moreover, real social welfare expenditures more than doubled to over $600 billion (1990 dollars) from 1964 to 1974 and almost doubled again by 1990. Public Aid, which includes the food stamp, school lunch, and Medicaid programmes, comprised about 15 per cent of this total, and it rose at a similar pace (Kimenyi, 1995: 318–19).

On the other hand, one could argue that even though poverty was not eliminated, it may have become less severe both in the aggregate as people move above the poverty threshold, and for individuals still in poverty whose income is raised. While data do not permit a comparison with 1964, column D in Table 31.1 shows the before-tax-and-transfer poverty rate and column E shows the after-tax and after-transfer (cash and non-cash) poverty rate for the 1979–88 period (Kimenyi, 1995: 322–3). The existence of social welfare programmes reduced the poverty rate significantly. However, the percentage reduction of people in

Table 31.1   US poverty rates and number of people in poverty, 1964–93

Year	A Official poverty rate for persons	B No. of people in poverty (millions)	C Real GDP per capita (1987 $)	D Poverty rate before taxes and transfers	E Poverty rate after taxes and transfers
1964	19.0	36.1	12 195		
1965	17.3	33.2	12 712		
1966	14.7	28.5	13 307		
1967	14.2	27.8	13 510		
1968	12.8	25.4	13 932		
1969	12.1	24.1	14 171		
1970	12.6	25.4	14 013		
1971	12.5	25.6	14 232		
1972	11.9	24.5	14 801		
1973	11.1	23.0	15 422		
1974	11.2	23.4	15 185		
1975	12.3	25.9	14 917		
1976	11.8	25.0	15 502		
1977	11.4	24.7	16 039		
1978	11.4	24.5	16 635		
1979	11.7	26.1	16 867	19.1	9.9
1980	13.0	29.3	16 584	20.6	11.6
1981	14.0	31.8	16 710	21.7	13.2
1982	15.0	34.4	16 194	22.6	14.2
1983	15.2	35.3	16 672	22.8	14.6
1984	14.4	33.7	17 549	21.8	13.9
1985	14.0	33.1	17 944	21.3	13.5
1986	13.6	32.4	18 299	20.8	13.1
1987	13.4	32.2	18 694	20.6	12.6
1988	13.0	31.7	19 252	20.2	12.0
1989	12.8	31.5	19 556		
1990	13.5	33.6	19 593		
1991	14.2	35.7	19 263		
1992	14.8	38.0	19 490		
1993	15.1	39.3	19 879		

Sources:
Columns A B and C from Council of Economic Advisors (1984; 1995).
Columns D and E from Kimenyi, (1995: 322–3).

poverty fluctuated from 48 per cent in 1979 declining to 36 per cent in 1983 and rising to 40+ per cent in 1988. This suggests that poverty reduction is not closely related to real social welfare expenditures, as the latter rose over the period. We can look at the *poverty gap* for persons, the difference between the aggregate of incomes of those in poverty before taxes and transfers and the aggregate of those in poverty after taxes are subtracted and transfers are added to income. The percentage reduction in the poverty gap was 71 per cent in 1979, declining to 66 per cent in 1983 and staying relatively flat after that with the 1993 mean poverty gap greater than in 1967 (Mishel and Bernstein, 1994: 261). With either measure, social insurance contributed over twice as much to the poverty gap reduction percentage as did means-tested transfers.

It is probable that the expansion and creation of government social welfare programmes have reduced poverty significantly below what it would be in the absence of such programmes, especially social security. However, with either the poverty rate or poverty gap measure there is no poverty reduction trend even though, as noted, real social welfare expenditures expanded significantly during that period (Kimenyi, 1995: 318–19). An important reason may be that benefits received by families did not rise over this period. Real monthly Aid to Families with Dependent Children (AFDC) benefits per family fell from 1969 to 1987 and real monthly benefits for AFDC, food stamps, and Medicaid combined fell from 1975, the first year data were available, until 1987 (Moffitt, 1992: 9).

What about the contribution of income growth to poverty reduction? We can get some idea about the contribution of real income growth to poverty reduction by looking at changes in real per capita GDP. In Table 31.1, column C, we see that from 1964 to 1974 real per capita GDP rose by over 24 per cent or 2.2 per cent compounded annually while the poverty rate in column A was falling by 41 per cent so real income growth may have been the major poverty reducer along with government tax and expenditure programmes. However, real GDP per capita also rose by 31 per cent or 1.4 per cent compounded annually from 1974 to 1993 while the poverty rate was rising by 35 per cent so its contribution to reducing poverty is, like welfare expenditures, confounding.

What causes poverty? Two approaches are evident: institutional, and rational individual. These are not necessarily mutually exclusive, but they provide alternative perspectives.

The *institutional approach* to poverty has two variants. One, associated with Karl Marx, sees poverty as a systematic part of capitalism, a

Table 31.2   US poverty rate and unemployment rate changes and female headship, 1964–92

Year	A Change in official poverty rate for families	B Change in rate of unemployment	C Proportion of families not in poverty headed by a female	D Proportion of families not in poverty headed by a female
1964	−0.9	−0.5	7.8	25.4
1965	−1.1	−0.7	7.3	28.5
1966	−2.1	−0.7	7.9	29.8
1967	−0.4	0.0	8.0	31.3
1968	−1.4	−0.2	8.0	34.8
1969	−0.3	−0.1	8.2	36.5
1970	+0.4	+1.4	8.6	37.1
1971	−0.1	+1.0	8.5	39.6
1972	−0.7	−0.3	9.0	42.5
1973	−0.5	−0.7	9.2	45.4
1974	0.0	+0.7	9.7	47.2
1975	+0.9	+2.9	9.9	44.6
1976	−0.3	−0.8	10.1	47.9
1977	−0.1	−0.6	10.8	49.1
1978	−0.2	−1.0	11.1	50.3
1979	+0.1	−0.3	11.2	48.4
1980	+1.1	+1.3	11.3	47.8
1981	+0.9	+0.5	11.4	47.5
1982	+1.0	+2.1	11.2	45.7
1983	+0.1	−0.1	11.6	46.6
1984	−0.7	−1.9	12.0	48.1
1985	−0.2	−0.3	12.0	48.1
1986	−0.5	−0.2	11.9	51.4
1987	−0.2	−0.8	12.1	52.2
1988	−0.3	−0.7	12.3	53.0
1989	−0.1	−0.2	12.5	51.7
1990	+0.4	+0.2	12.7	53.1
1991	+0.8	+1.2	12.7	54.0
1992	+0.2	+0.7	12.9	52.4

Sources:
Column B from Council of Economic Advisors (1984; 1995).
Columns A, C and D from US Department of Commerce (1992), p. xiv.

necessary result of the way a capitalist system is structured and develops within a class-consciousness. In this view poverty follows necessarily from the greater political power of the owners of capital as compared to workers, and institutions are created to perpetuate this power. Two of these structures are the dual labour market and the welfare system. The primary sector requires high skill levels and generates high wages, good benefits and working conditions, low unemployment, and potential for advancement. In contrast, the secondary sector requires low skills and generates low wages, few benefits and poor working conditions, high unemployment and little chance of advancement. Upward movement from the secondary to the primary sector is unusual because of the much higher education requirements in the primary sector, management practice of sex and race discrimination, and the secondary sector labour culture which generates poor work habits, short-run planning horizons, and low self-esteem among workers. Females and racial minorities – Afro-Americans, Hispanics and Native Americans – are disproportionally represented in the secondary sector which consists of jobs such as retail sales, fast food, and unskilled construction work (Carson, 1987: 187–90). Management attitudes toward females and minorities are shaped by the gender and race structure of the workplace, and they are seen as less capable than workers in the primary sector. In addition management may exploit sex and race discrimination among workers themselves to weaken worker solidarity and prevent unionization, to create a pool of reserve labour that can be hired and fired as needed (Hunt and Sherman, 1986: 367–8). The culture of poverty produces political pressure for welfare which benefits corporate America as well as the poor, as the poor are enabled to buy more products. The welfare system, in this view, slows the momentum but not the direction of poverty growth over time, preserving welfare capitalism while keeping the poor locked in a kind of social bondage as they look to government for solutions to their poverty instead of seeing the systematic labour segmentation and discrimination that produces poverty as inherent in capitalism itself. Since the systematic variant of institutionalism assesses society in broad terms, it does not lend itself to specific testing. Evidence which broadly supports the systematic view of poverty in the USA includes the growth of the number of people in poverty over time, the failure of benefits to those in poverty to grow over time, the increase in income inequality over the last 30 years (Kimenyi, 1995: 82), the failure of the poverty gap to narrow, and the stronger unions and higher income shares associated with markets that reveal less discrimination (Kimenyi, 1995: 213). Evidence which does not support this view includes the reduction in unemployment for females compared to males (Kimenyi, 1995: 197).

The other variant of the *institutional approach* to poverty sees specific institutions as producing or perpetuating poverty, but does not see these as deriving from class-consciousness and moulded by class power struggles. In fact it tends to eschew an overarching explanation for poverty, focusing instead on the specific nature of institutions such as dual labour markets and looking for contextual variations. It focuses on identifying information that would better aid understanding the workings of these institutions that individuals must deal with in a specific time and place and which significantly constrain their behaviour in avoiding or leaving poverty. Institutional reasons for poverty include high unemployment, low wages, sex and race discrimination, family structure, age-related factors, the nature of the welfare system, and the culture of poverty that shapes behaviour.

Unemployment and the absence of employment opportunities is an important source of poverty in the USA. Cyclical unemployment, caused by a downturn in the business cycle, and structural unemployment, caused by worker skills failing to correlate to available jobs, create most unemployment. The relationship of unemployment to poverty can be seen by the change in the unemployment rate in column B in Table 31.2 being positively correlated with the change in the poverty rate in column A in Table 31.2. This relationship is weaker for single mothers and was less strong in the 1980s because many jobs created were low-wage jobs, another cause of poverty (Kimenyi, 1995: 124–7). Low wages, perpetuated by dual labour markets, also contribute to the poverty rate, as over a third of those in poverty worked full-time in 1987 (Kimenyi, 1995: 144). Unemployment rates and median incomes of Afro-Americans, Hispanics and Native Americans are significantly higher that those of Caucasians. Median incomes of women are significantly lower than those of males (Kimenyi, 1995: 194–201). Since these group differences could be due to characteristics such as age, education, experience and location, regression studies have been designed to see if these characteristics explain most of the differential in wages for these groups. If they do then economic discrimination – the refusal to hire a person who is more qualified than others – is not significant. What these studies show is that about 50 per cent of the black/white wage differential and 10 per cent of the male/female wage differential are left unexplained, which, by implication, become measures of economic discrimination (Kimenyi, 1995: 202).

Family structure is also important. A high proportion of families headed by a single mother are in poverty. The proportion has been rising over time as Table 31.2, columns C and D, show, and divorce/ separation and out-of-wedlock births are the primary reasons for the increase. From 1960 to 1988 the percentage of black children not living with two parents had risen from 33 per cent to 61 per cent, and the proportion of black children born to an unmarried mother had risen from 23 per cent to over 60 per cent (Ellwood and Crane, 1990: 65). The poverty rate for two-parent black families with children was 12.5 per cent in 1988 while for single-parent black families with children it was 56 per cent in 1989 (Ellwood and Crane, 70).

Another reason for poverty is age. Teenagers have few skills and no experience and if they are independent, they can easily be below the poverty line. Over 20 per cent of them are in poverty. Also, people are living longer and have more years of heavy health expenditures than in the past. If they do not anticipate their longevity, they may not save enough or assume that social security will be adequate, thus putting themselves into poverty. Over 10 per cent of the people over 65 are in poverty but this figure is much reduced from earlier years due to the rising levels of social security (Kimenyi, 1995: 110).

The nature of the welfare system may also contribute to poverty or not alleviate it as much as it could by subtracting welfare benefits for each dollar earned at rates approaching 100 per cent (Moffitt, 1992: 10) and by creating so much red tape and structure that only those poor who can figure out how the system works benefit from it. The culture of poverty that one grows up in creates an environment that produces an attitude not conducive to gaining and retaining a job. This attitude includes a lack of motivation, lack of interest in education, a low level of independence, and a poor work ethic (Kimenyi, 1995: 113). Consequently, such workers do not respond to the normal economic incentives, and welfare programmes designed, as was the 'War on Poverty', to create worker self-sufficiency do not work. The 'War on Poverty' attempted to develop programmes that would create self-sufficiency, not dependency, so this is a serious issue. AFDC studies indicate that while there is a great deal of variability among subgroups, mean duration of AFDC recipiency is about five years, and at least a fifth of recipients will have welfare careers of eight or nine years (Kimenyi, 1995: 355).

In contrast to the institutional approach which places the primary explanation for poverty on society and its institutions, the *rational individual approach* to poverty assumes that economically rational individuals respond to the rewards and penalties of the economic system so as to improve their material well-being. The focus is on how individuals choose, subject to institutional constraints, not on how institutional constraints shape individual choice.

This approach makes poverty, for some individuals, a conscious choice. That is, individuals choose a work–leisure tradeoff such that so little work is done that, given their low skill level, these individuals earn an income below the poverty line. Such individuals may also not be willing to invest in the education and training needed to improve their material well-being. If we add a welfare system as an alternative to work, some individuals may choose to behave in such a way as to make them welfare recipients because this choice maximizes their utility given their work–leisure tradeoff. Much of the thinking about poverty from this perspective has focused on the effects of the welfare system on individual choice and whether it serves to increase poverty and reduce work effort in the aggregate. Charles Murray's book, *Losing Ground* (1984), has been important in guiding a political agenda aimed at reducing the welfare system based on this perspective. The key issues involve the effect of the welfare system on labour supply or work effort, welfare participation and turnover, family structural changes, migration from less attractive to more attractive welfare locations, and future generation welfare recipiency (Moffitt, 1992: 2).

The existence of a welfare programme provides a minimum level of guaranteed income and with participation imposes a benefit reduction 'tax' on wage earning. Concern has been with whether or not hours of work effort have been reduced by the existence and evolution of welfare programmes. The average welfare benefit of AFDC across states approximates what one would earn if one worked full-time at a minimum wage, although benefit levels vary significantly from state to state. Consequently, the disincentive effect of AFDC on labour supply is not trivial and is estimated at five to six hours per week, which amounts to about a 30 per cent work effort reduction since most AFDC recipients would be working less that 20 hours per week if they did not get AFDC. However, very little of this labour supply reduction comes from initially ineligible female heads who lower their hours of work to become eligible for AFDC, so that the labour force participation rate is reduced only 3–4 per cent by its existence. The labour supply effects of other transfer programmes (food stamps, Medicaid, housing assistance) have not been sufficiently investigated to draw believable conclusions, and this important work needs to be done (Moffitt, 1992: 15–19). Empirical models examining participation in AFDC have tended to find what the rational individual model predicts – that the probability of participation is positively related to the level of benefits, and negatively related to the benefit tax rate and hourly wage rates.

Exit from AFDC has also been found to be negatively related to the level of benefits. Empirical studies also indicate that while almost 50 per cent of new AFDC periods last less than two years (a year being defined as receiving at least one month of benefits sometime during the year), re-entry is common and almost 25 per cent of new AFDC recipients will spend ten or more years on AFDC, lending some credence to the notion of a 'culture of poverty' (Moffitt, 1992: 19–27).

Evidence also shows that most entry into and exit from AFDC is associated with changes in family structure and not with changes in labour effort or earnings. Because AFDC benefits primarily go to female-only family heads, the rational individual perspective sees AFDC benefit changes as providing incentives to delay marriage and remarriage, increase divorce and separation and have children (since the benefit level goes up by number of children). Cross-section econometric evidence is not very supportive of these hypotheses in the 1960s and 1970s and only slightly supportive for the 1980s. Interestingly, simple observation of the 1964–75 period tends to support the occurrence of these effects. However, as benefit levels declined in the late 1970s and 1980s, only the divorce rate for the whole population decreased as would be predicted from the model, but divorces for those not in poverty are obviously not affected by AFDC benefit changes. After 1975 both white and non-white female headship continued to grow, birth rates fell, and white illegitimacy grew while non-white illegitimacy fell slightly, a result not consistent with the rational individual model. Marriage is less likely to take place before a birth for reasons that do not seem to be connected to the welfare system. One possible explanation is that there has been an increasing scarcity of economically suitable partners (Moffitt, 1992: 27–31). While it is clear that there has been a rapid change in the structure of poor families, it is not clear that changes in welfare benefit levels contributed much to it by making poverty and more children an attractive economic option. While the percentage of black children not living with two parents rose steadily by 28 per cent over the 1960–88 period, welfare benefits revealed a different pattern. Real AFDC and food stamp payment levels rose from 1960 to 1970 by 35 per cent but fell 22 per cent from 1970 to 1988. Also, the estimated percentage of black children in families collecting AFDC rose by 23.2 per cent in the earlier period and fell by 10 per cent from 1970 to 1988 (Ellwood and Crane, 1990: 72–4). Thus it does not appear that the changing family structure was motivated by the desire to acquire welfare benefits. Summarizing a number of studies, Ellwood and Crane conclude that there may be effects of welfare on family structure, but they are not strong (Ellwood and Crane, 74).

Do benefit levels across states relate positively to AFDC participation levels, as the rational individual model predicts? Here recent studies show positive and significant effects of welfare on residential location and geographic mobility, but causal conclusions are not warranted because the cross-sectional nature of the data does not necessarily indicate that anyone *moved* from one location to another to obtain higher AFDC benefits, which is the hypothesis of interest.

Are future generations affected by the current welfare structure in that growing up in a welfare household could induce a 'taste' for welfare along with the knowledge of how to utilize the welfare system effectively, or that family or one's own investment in human capital is affected by the existence of welfare? The available empirical studies show a high and significant positive correlation between parental welfare receipt and their daughters' later participation in the welfare system, birth rates, and illegitimate births, although it is weaker for sons' labour market performance. Unfortunately, none of these studies control for omitted variables that could be responsible for the observed correlation, such as the education of the parental family (Moffitt, 1992: 36–40), and so believable conclusions are not possible.

What then can we conclude about the poverty puzzle? There is no dearth of explanations for poverty in the USA. A major problem is that the evidence we have is not strongly supportive of any of them. A more significant problem is that the data have not been gathered and the studies have not been done which could help unravel this important and difficult puzzle. The complexity of the puzzle can be seen in a different way.

A family will tend to be in poverty when its members have an inadequate income. From an individual's perspective what would contribute to earning an inadequate income? These non-homogeneous factors would be included: the lack of appropriate innate talents, the absence of motivation, the lack of appropriate knowledge (about ideas, people, things, processes), the absence of appropriate resources owned or controlled, bad luck, and an inadequate social climate for economic betterment (weak property rights structure, anti-material societal attitudes such as sex, race, and religious discrimination). If we agree that each of these factors is under varying degrees of control by the individual or family, this makes analysis of poverty from either a solely individualistic or institutional perspective very incomplete and shallow. It also makes formulating solutions to poverty complex and uncertain, which makes generating public policy measures that the public can understand problematic. The poverty puzzle remains and is likely to do so for the foreseeable future.

K.C.T.

REFERENCES

Carson, Robert B. (1987), *Economic Issues Today – Alternative Approaches*, 4th edn, New York: St Martin's Press.
Council of Economic Advisors (1984; 1995), *Economic Report(s) of the President*.
Ellwood, David T. and Jonathan Crane (1990), 'Family Change Among Black Americans: What Do We Know?' *Journal of Economic Perspectives*, **4** (4), 65–84.
Hunt, E.K. and H. J. Sherman (1986), *Economics – An Introduction to Traditional and Radical Views*, 5th edn, New York: Harper & Row, ch. 25.
Kimenyi, Mwangi S. (1995), *Economics of Poverty, Discrimination and Public Policy*, Cincinnati, Ohio: South-Western College Publishing, chs 4 and 5.
Mishel, Lawrence and Jared Bernstein, (1994), *The State of Working America 1994–95*, Economic Policy Institute, New York: M.E. Sharpe, ch. 6.
Moffitt, Robert (1992), 'The Incentive Effects of the U.S. Welfare System: A Review', *Journal of Economic Literature*, **30**, 1–61.
Murray, Charles (1984), *Losing Ground – American Social Policy 1950–1980*, New York: Basic Books.
US Department of Commerce (various years), *Current Population Reports*, Series P-60.
US Department of Commerce, Bureau of the Census (1992), *Poverty in the United States: 1992*, Series P-60–185.
US Department of Commerce, Bureau of the Census (1995) *Statistical Abstract of the USA*, 1995.

32. The paradox of thrift

The classic textbook case, where greater thriftiness reduces spending, forces business to cut back production, which in turn lays off workers, reduces income and ultimately reduces saving. 'While savings may pave the road to riches for an individual, if the nation as a whole decides to save more, the result may be a recession and poverty for all' (Baumol and Blinder, 1988: 192). How can the paradox of thrift be resolved?

The paradox of thrift has led many economists to adopt an anti-saving mentality, particularly during downturns in the economy when business and consumers turn pessimistic. Much of this anti-thrift doctrine developed during the Great Depression of the 1930s, when many consumers stopped buying, cash was often hoarded and banks built up cash balances. E.F.M. Durbin summarized the underconsumptionist attack on savings as follows:

> Saving is a peculiarly dangerous and self-defeating process, for it withdraws money from the purchase of finished commodities and makes their production less profitable, while at the same time it seeks to set up still further capital resources with which the production of finished commodities is to be increased. It is this paradoxical process which makes a deficiency of purchasing power inevitable. It increases the supply of and diminishes the demand for the products of the industrial system to the point at which production cannot be continued any longer with profit and at that point crisis and depression begin. Hence depression can always be prevented and relieved either by reducing the amount of saving or by stimulating consumption by the issue of new money. (Durbin, 1933: 22)

During the Depression, John Maynard Keynes lashed out at frugal savers and hoarders. In a radio broadcast in January 1931, he asserted that thriftiness would cause a 'vicious circle' of poverty,

> For the object of saving is to release labour for employment on producing capital-goods such as houses, factories, roads, machines, and the like. But if there is a large unemployed surplus already available for such purposes, then the effect of saving is merely to add to this surplus and therefore to increase the number of unemployed.

He bluntly told his audience that if 'you save five shillings, you put a man out of work for a day' (Keynes, 1963: 152).

The paradox of thrift became a mainstay of Keynesian economic thinking through the publication of Paul A. Samuelson's popular textbook, *Economics*. Samuelson expressed the constant fear that an increased propensity to save may 'leak' out of the system and 'become a social vice' (Samuelson, 1948: 253). According to the saving–investment schedule (the Keynesian cross), saving was only a virtue at times of full employment. At less than full employment, there existed a paradox of thrift. 'When this is the case, everything goes into reverse.' According to Samuelson, the classical model became perverse, wherein increased saving reduces rather than increases wealth and investment. Saving was sometimes referred to as 'hoarding' (Samuelson, 1948: 271).

Except for the fourteenth edition, Samuelson has included the paradox of thrift section in all editions of his textbook. Using the Keynesian saving-and-investment figure (see Figure 32.1), Samuelson illustrates the paradox of thrift:

In an underemployed economy, desire to consume less at every income

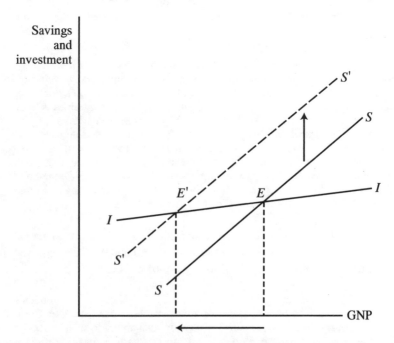

Figure 32.1   Samuelson's paradox of thrift

level will shift the savings schedule upward. With the II curve unchanged, equilibrium drops to the E′ prime intersection. Why? Because income has to fall – and fall in a multiplied way – until people feel poor enough so that they again want to save the amount of planned investment at II. (Samuelson and Nordhaus, 1989: 184)

Samuelson 'resolves' the paradox by arguing that the only time thrift is a virtue is during full employment, when 'output could be assumed to be always at its potential'.

Other Keynesians have joined Samuelson in condemning saving during times of unemployed resources. The quote from William J. Baumol's and Alan S. Blinder's textbook is stated above (Baumol and Blinder, 1988: 192).

Is Samuelson anti-saving all the time or just occasionally? Throughout his editions, he tended to be pro-saving when the economy was at full employment, and anti-saving when it was underemployed. 'But full employment and inflationary conditions have occurred only occasionally in our recent history. Much of the time there is some wastage of resources, some unemployment, some insufficiency of demand, investment, and purchasing power' (Samuelson, 1948: 271). This paragraph remained virtually the same throughout the first eleven editions (see, for example, eleventh edition, 1980: 226). In sum, Samuelson was almost always anti-thrift, at least until the twelfth edition.

In this regard, his personal financial advice in his textbook appeared risky. 'Never again can people be urged in times of depression to tighten their belts, to save more in order to restore prosperity. The result will be just the reverse – a worsening of the vicious deflationary spiral' (1948; 272; 1980: 227). In the third edition, Samuelson denounced families which 'hysterically cut down on consumption when economic clouds arise' (1955: 339). In a later edition he echoed the advice of Harvard economist Frank W. Taussig, who during the Great Depression went on the radio 'to urge everyone to save less, to spend more on consumption' (1967: 226). He appeared to have little sympathy toward disciplined individuals and businesses which watched their expenses closely, built a strong cash position, and avoided debt during a recession.

PROGRESSIVE TAXATION

Samuelson's anti-thrift model extended to his discussion on progressive taxation and the 'balanced-budget multiplier'. One of the 'favourable' effects of progressive taxation was stated as follows: 'To the extent that dollars are taken from frugal wealthy people rather than from poor ready spenders, progressive taxes tend to keep purchasing power and jobs at a high level – perhaps at too high a level if inflation is threatening' (1948: 174; 1980: 161). Samuelson implied that a high level of consumption, not a high level of saving, would be the key to prosperity.

BALANCED-BUDGET MULTIPLIER

Anti-thrift dogma came through also in the 'balanced-budget multiplier' theorem of the 'income determination' model. Samuelson stated: 'Hence, dollars of tax reduction are almost as powerful a weapon against mass unemployment as are increases in dollars of government expenditure' (1967: 234; 1980; 232). Why 'almost'? Because only a portion of the tax cut would be 'spent' (the rest would be saved) by the public, whereas all government expenditures would be spent. The model implied that saving was not spending, but might be hoarded or end up in excessive cash balances at the bank. The 'balanced-budget multiplier' seemed to apply only to a 'depression' situation.

THE DECLINE IN THE 'PARADOX OF THRIFT'

Has Samuelson's anti-saving mentality changed over the years? A figure similar to Figure 32.1, showing saving leaking out of the economic system, was published in every edition until the thirteenth (1989). The 'paradox of thrift' doctrine had remained a principal feature in all the editions until then. In the thirteenth edition, co-authored by Nordhaus, the 'paradox of thrift' section was made optional (1989: 183–5). Then in the fourteenth edition, it was removed entirely.

Samuelson reversed himself again, however, in the fifteenth edition (1995), reinserting the 'paradox of thrift' material (1995: 455–7). He stated, 'economists who wish to encourage consumption rather than saving in recessions do so not because they are opposed to investment but because they may believe that by stimulating consumption there will be more output to devote to investment' (1995: 457). Samuelson justified his decision: 'Disappearing to zero was, in my reconsidered judgment, an overshoot' (Personal correspondence, 20 January 1995). He claimed that Japan in 1992–94 could be a modern-day example of the paradox of thrift. Nordhaus pointed to Europe in the early 1990s and America in the early 1980s as potential examples (Private correspondence, 4 February 1995).

Yet there is growing evidence that Samuelson's heart is no longer in it. Beginning with the thirteenth edition (1989), a major pro-savings section was added. It bemoaned the gradual decline in the savings rate in the USA (1989: 142–4). Samuelson and Nordhaus asserted a strong correlation between the rate of savings and economic growth. '... virtually all [macroeconomists] believe that the savings rate is too low to guarantee a vital and healthy rate of investment in the 1990s' (1989: 144). They listed several potential causes of low savings: federal budget deficits, social security, high inflation and high taxes.

INCREASE INVESTMENT THROUGH GROWTH, NOT THRIFT

Given their anti-saving bias, how do Keynesians stimulate saving and investment, which everyone agrees is the key to long-term economic growth? Franco Modigliani argues that the 'key to saving is growth, not thrift'. He uses postwar Japan as an example:

One of the interesting implications of the life-cycle theory suggests that when a country needs capital to drive rapid growth, capital will be forthcoming. The growth process itself generates saving. Once Japan's growth engine got going, it produced enormous saving, at times amounting to one quarter of annual national income. (Modigliani, 1987: 24)

Robert Eisner, who calls himself an 'unreconstructed Keynesian', argues similarly: 'To raise the saving rate, try spending.' The key to more investment is a high-consumption society. 'Investing in education and public works will boost savings' (Eisner, 1988).

Gregory Mankiw represents a more modern Keynesian attitude toward saving by starting with the long-run classical position in his textbook, *Macroeconomics* (1994). In his chapter on economic growth, he focuses on the Solow model, where the saving rate is 'a key determinant of the steady-state capital stock'. Furthermore, 'Higher saving leads to faster growth, but only in the short run' (Mankiw, 1994: 86). Clearly, this approach is quite different from Samuelson's and that of the early Keynesians.

RESOLVING THE PARADOX OF THRIFT

The paradox-of-thrift doctrine has been criticized by neoclassical and Austrian economists. Axel Leijonhufvud labels the Keynesian anti-saving doctrine 'one of the most dangerous and harmful confusions ever taught as accepted economic doctrine' (Leijonhufvud, 1981: 197). James Akiakpor argues that Keynes inappropriately defined savings as hoarding of cash, 'contrary to the classical definition which limits saving to the purchase of interest- or profit-earning assets' (Akiakpor, 1995: 28). Samuelson, I might add, goes even further, defining saving as 'not spending'. Thus, Keynes and the Keynesians contradict 'the classical saving theory of growth'. If saving is invested rather than hoarded, the paradox of thrift 'disappears' (Akiakpor, 1995: 30).

Friedrich A. von Hayek and other Austrian economists dispute the Keynesians' notion that economic growth is dependent on increased consumer demand rather than increased savings. Increased saving may initially reduce final consumer demand, but it increases the demand for higher-order capital goods through a reduced interest rate. Total spending in the economy, therefore, does not decline. A fall in interest rates increases the demand for capital goods, so that businesses can now afford to expand facilities, build new plants, buy new tools and equipment, and engage in research and development. The problem, according to Hayek, is that the Keynesian macro theory is essentially a two-stage model, where the demand for investment is dependent entirely on the demand for consumption. In reality, the economy consists of multi-stages of intertemporal processes, so that a decline in the final consumer stage is offset by a rise in the higher stages of production (Hayek, 1939; Skousen, 1990: 241–64).

Keynesians emphasize the role of business and consumer expectations during the business cycle. If expectations are pessimistic, lower interest rates may not have the stimulative effect expected. Government may have to intervene.

A NEOCLASSICAL SYNTHESIS

Following the lines of Modigliani and Mankiw, there is a way to complement both the Keynesian, classical and Austrian positions on saving. Encourage both saving and consumer spending during periods of economic growth. As real income rises for both individuals and firms, economists could advocate that individuals spend some of their additional income on consumption goods and invest a substantial part in financial assets and bank deposits. Firms would also be encouraged to retain much of their earnings to reinvest in plant, equipment, research and development and employee training, while paying the remainder in dividends to shareholders. That way consumer spending rises and so does saving and investing. The result would be a new spirit of economic growth.

However, during an economic downturn, classical economists and Keynesians are likely to remain at odds, with classical and Austrian economists favouring liquidity and cost-cutting measures and Keynesians advocating priming the pump to restore consumer and business confidence.

M.S.

REFERENCES

Akiakpor, James C.W. (1995), 'A Paradox of Thrift or Keynes's Misrepresentation of Saving in the Classical Theory of Growth?', *Southern Economic Journal*, July, 16–33.

Baumol, William J. and Alan S. Blinder (1988), *Economics: Principles and Policy*, 4th edn, New York: Harcourt Brace Jovanovich.

Durbin, E.F.M. (1933), *Purchasing Power and the Trade Depression*, London: Jonathan Cape.

Eisner, Robert (1988), 'To Raise the Saving Rate, Try Spending', *New York Times* (op-ed page, 29 August).

Hayek, Friedrich A. von (1939), 'The "Paradox" of Saving' in *Profits, Interest and Investment*, London: George Routledge & Sons, pp. 199–263.

Keynes, John Maynard (1963), *Essays in Persuasion*, New York: W.W. Norton.

Leijonhufvud, Axel (1981), *Information and Coordination*, New York: Oxford University Press.

Mankiw, N. Gregory (1994), *Macroeconomics*, 2nd edn, New York: Worth Publishers.

Modigliani, Franco (1987), 'The Key to Saving is Growth, Not Thrift,' *Challenge*, May–June.

Samuelson, Paul A. (1948), *Economics*, New York: McGraw-Hill. Later editions are referred to by date: 1955, 1967, 1980 and 1995.

Samuelson, Paul A. and William D. Nordhaus (1989), *Economics*, New York: McGraw-Hill.

Skousen, Mark (1990), *The Structure of Production*, New York: New York University Press.

33.   The gold absurdity

Paul Samuelson declares, 'How absurd to waste resources digging gold out of the bowels of the earth, only to inter it back again in the vaults of Fort Knox, Kentucky!' (Samuelson, 1970: 700). How can this apparent absurdity under a gold standard be rationalized?

Samuelson expresses the conventional wisdom regarding the high cost involved with a monetary system under gold. A commodity standard is viewed as a waste of resources. Other economists have expressed similar sentiments. Roy J. Ruffin and Paul R. Gregory state, 'It also seems unwise to dig up gold and then turn around and bury it again in Fort Knox, all for the purpose of restraining the growth of the money supply' (Ruffin and Gregory, 1988: 316).

Milton Friedman estimated that the cost of a pure commodity standard would be around 4 per cent of the annual GDP, the amount of real resources devoted to mining in order to increase the stock of money and keep prices fairly constant. 'The use of so large a volume of resources for this purpose establishes a strong social incentive in a growing economy to find cheaper ways to provide a medium of exchange' (Friedman, 1960: 5–7). Historically, however, gold production has seldom increased the monetary stock of gold beyond 2 per cent a year. Nevertheless, it does represent a large volume of resources devoted to mining the precious metal.

Surprisingly, Ludwig von Mises, Friedrich von Hayek, and other Austrian economists who support the gold standard for political reasons, accept this economic argument against gold (Skousen, 1996).

However, in recent years, a new response against the waste-of-resources argument has appeared. This argument states that even without a gold standard (since 1971) the cost of mining and storing gold has not disappeared. Roger Garrison was the first to make this point: 'The imposition of a paper standard does not cause gold to lose its monetary value . . . Gold continues to be mined, refined, cast or minted, stored, and guarded; the resource costs continue to be incurred' (Garrison, 1985: 70). In fact, Garrison argues that the government's propensity to inflate and destabilize its own fiat-money system may encourage artificially higher levels of resources devoted to exploration, extraction and refining of precious metals. Indeed, the government minting and trading of gold coins have increased dramatically since the early 1970s, when the world went off the international gold standard. As a result, more gold is being extracted and reburied in vaults as never before – perhaps not in the vaults of Fort Knox, but in the vaults of commercial institutions and private individuals.

In response to Garrison's argument, Milton Friedman has reversed his position on the cost-of-resource argument (although Friedman still considers a gold standard unworkable):

> Yet the resource cost has not been eliminated; it remains present because private individuals hoard precious metals and gold and silver coins as a hedge against inflation that they fear may result from a wholly fiduciary money. To go farther afield, a new resource cost has been added because a purely fiduciary currency reduces the long-run predictability of the price level. (Friedman and Schwartz, 1987: 310)

Friedman summarizes, 'Our own conclusion – like that of Walter Bagehot and Vera Smith – is that leaving monetary and banking arrangements to the market would have produced a more satisfactory outcome than was actually achieved through government involvement' (Friedman and Schwartz, 1987: 311).

In short, the monetary ritual of unearthing and interring gold reflects a constant demand by individuals to maintain assets that preserve their value over the centuries.

M.S.

REFERENCES

Friedman, Milton (1960), *A Program for Monetary Stability*, New York: Fordham University Press.

Friedman, Milton and Anna J. Schwartz (1987), 'Has Government Any Role in Money?', in Anna J. Schwartz, *Money in Historical Perspective*, Chicago, Illinois: University of Chicago Press, pp. 289–314. This article originally appeared in the *Journal of Monetary Economics*, January 1986.

Garrison, Roger W. (1985), 'The Cost of a Gold Standard', in Llewellyn H. Rockwell, Jr (ed.), *The Gold Standard*, Lexington, Massachusetts: Lexington Books, pp. 61–80.

Ruffin, Roy J. and Paul R. Gregory (1988), *Principles of Economics*, 3rd edn, Glenview, Illinois: Scott, Foreman.

Samuelson, Paul A. (1970), *Economics*, 7th edn, New York: McGraw-Hill.

Skousen, Mark (1996), *Economics of a Pure Gold Standard*, 3rd edn, New York: Foundation for Economic Education.

34. The wager over wages

In 1914, Henry Ford tripled the average wage at his auto factory to $5 a day. Ford hired new workers and productivity and profits both increased substantially. In 1930, Ford raised wages (in real terms), but profits fell, and Ford had to lay off workers. How can you explain this difference in outcome?

To understand the difference between these two events, we must consider the historical background, and note in particular the intertemporal relationship between the payment of wages and the earning of profits.

In the early 1910s, the Ford Motor Company was the most successful automobile company in the world. Sales of the Model T grew from 5986 to 78 611 units in 1912. In 1913 Ford's total sales rose from $42 million to $89 million. Net income doubled from $13.5 million to $27 million, and net assets grew from $21 million to $35 million (Hughes, 1986: 301).

With such huge profits, Ford decided to share his gains with his employees. At the time, the minimum wage was $2 a day. In January 1914, at a board meeting, Ford proposed to increase the minimum wage paid to his Detroit workers. For four hours, the board members discussed how profits would be affected by wage increases. Charles Sorensen wrote on a blackboard a computation of cost, sales and profit data based on wage step increases of 25 cents from the existing range of $2 to $2.50 until $5 was reached. Finally, Ford exclaimed, 'Stop it Charlie, it's all settled. Five dollars a day minimum and at once' (Hughes, 1986: 302). Thus was born the famous Five Dollar Day story, which made Henry Ford an industrial Messiah.

The effect of the instant pay rise was dramatic. There was a tremendous surge in output and skyrocketing morale among Ford workers. Thousands of potential employees moved to Detroit in hopes of getting a job. Ford argued that the higher wage had two great benefits: increased efficiency at the automobile plant, and increased buying power of his workers. Importantly, the $5 wage permitted Ford workers to buy the cars they were making for the first time. Ford stated, 'If we can distribute high wages, then the money is going to be spent and it will serve to make storekeepers and distributors and manufacturers and workers on other lines more prosperous, and their prosperity will be reflected in our sales' (Ford, 1923: 124). Indeed, sales of Model Ts continued to soar as wages went up and prices declined. By 1916, over half a million cars were sold.

Following this experience, Ford became a champion of 'vulgar Keynesianism', suggesting that the higher the national wage bill, the more money consumers would be prepared to spend.

However, Ford's purchasing power theory was challenged following the stock market crash of 1929. On 21 November 1929, President Herbert Hoover called a White House conference and invited Henry Ford and many other industrial leaders to deal with a possible depression. Hoover encouraged these business leaders to maintain real wages during the downturn. Ford was determined to cooperate, and even raised wages temporarily. But his scheme ultimately failed. Sales of his Model A sagged, and he was eventually forced to cut wages. He declared, 'Country-wide high wages spell country-wide prosperity, provided, however, the higher wages are paid from higher production' (quoted in Hughes, 1986: 305).

There are two reasons why Ford's wage plan worked in 1914 but failed in 1930. First, a 'micro' explanation. Ford paid out more wages that theoretically could be used to buy more cars. In 1914, Ford workers did indeed use the extra income to purchase Model Ts. But in 1930, Ford workers may have chosen otherwise. They may have used their new income to buy other products, or because of the impending recession, to save the money rather than spend it. In short, with sales lagging in 1930, the Ford Motor Company was taking a high risk that extra wage income would be spent on their products rather than on other products. In sum, the micro effects are not always the same as the macro effects.

Second, the 'time' factor. Ford could afford to double his employees' wages in 1914 because he had earned sufficient profits to do so in 1913. Profits preceded wage hikes. But the situation was entirely different in 1930. In 1930, the economy had slid into recession, and there were no excess profits to pay higher wages, creating a cost squeeze during this time. While Ford paid out higher wages immediately, he had to wait for higher sales in the future. Frederick C. Mills explains this time factor as follows:

> In a money economy a large portion of the sums that represent disbursements of purchasing power on the one hand represents costs on the other. Salaries and wages on the producers' account books are costs, and must be covered by receipts from the sales of good produced. If we could ignore the

time lag involved we might say that in a completely closed system, in which disbursements representing costs of production went to precisely the group of persons who constitute the final market for the good produced, whether costs (and related prices) stood on high or low levels would be a matter of indifference as regards the current movements of goods. But when the disbursements go to a smaller group than those who buy the products, or a different group, the relative levels of costs and of prices may be of profound importance. For the prices necessary to cover higher disbursements may be too high, in relation to the current income of the consuming group at large. Under these conditions an advance in costs and in prices may reduce the physical volume of goods sold, or impede expansion. (Mills, 1936: 397–8)

M.S.

REFERENCES

Ford, Henry (1923), *My Life and Work*, Garden City, New York: Doubleday.
Hughes, Jonathan (1986), *The Vital Few*, New York: Oxford University Press.
Mills, Frederick C. (1936), *Prices in Recession and Recovery*, New York: National Bureau of Economic Research.

35. The voting behaviour puzzle

Since the probability of influencing an election by one's vote is virtually nil, and the cost of gaining useful information about the candidates is quite high, the act of voting seems to be irrational. Yet millions of people, some of them of obvious intelligence, and some of them well informed, do vote in national, state and local elections. How can we explain this puzzle?

An important assumption of the *public choice* theory of political behaviour (Downs, 1957) is that people who act in the public sector (voters, politicians, special interest groups, bureaucrats) behave in the same way as people in the private sector (business people, consumers, workers). That is, they are *economically rational*. This means that they make consistent choices directed toward well-defined goals, and these are largely materially driven and egoistic. People who consider whether or not to vote do so to maximize their expected material satisfaction. With the voting decision framed in this way, incentives are such that people would not vote. This approach is often contrasted with the *public interest* theory of political behaviour wherein political agents are assumed to act for the good of society, and voting is taken to be a normal part of one's civic duty.

The public interest approach sees voting for political candidates as the norm, and the failure of a substantial majority to vote as symptomatic of sociopolitical problems in a democratic society, such as disaffection with political candidates or the decline of civic responsibility among the populace. This view is problematic for three reasons. First, in many voting situations, including US presidential elections, a majority of the public eligible to vote may not do so (Browning and Browning, 1987: 68). Public interest theory should be able to explain disaffection with politicians and the absence of civic responsibility if voting behaviour is to be understood at all. However, there is no public interest theory in which such behaviour is central to an understanding of voting behaviour. Second, these attitude variables can only be measured by surveys, and since surveys are subject to a variety of biases that are difficult to avoid, reliability is questionable. Third, this view suggests that there is a permanent problem with democracy by majority vote. Consequently many, though not all, mainstream economists have opted for another approach, called public choice theory. This approach is appealing in that it looks at material incentives to vote from an individual's perspective and employs a benefit–cost framework to assess tradeoffs. Both incentives and tradeoffs form core elements of mainstream economic theory and lend themselves to measurement, at least in principle.

Using public choice theory, no presumption about normal voting behaviour is made. Instead, an economically rational person is assumed to compare the personal material costs of voting with the personal material benefits of voting, in much the way as a person in the private market would compare the cost of a good with the benefits received from the services of that good. A major difference between the vote you cast for a candidate in the public sector and the dollar vote you expend for a good in the private sector is that in the private sector, the dollar vote you expend gives you control over the item acquired while the political vote you cast is diluted by others who vote. In terms of election outcomes, your vote only matters trivially. Even if the majority choice turns out to be yours, the votes cast by the chosen candidate after the election will probably not correspond closely to your perception of his views before the election because of the difficulty of assessing a candidate's views (Buchanan and Tullock, 1962: 36–9). To put it differently, voters will choose to remain partially ignorant about issues and candidates because of the time and effort costs of becoming well informed and the knowledge that even if one does become well informed, one's voting power is negligible anyway. Also, the candidate chosen cannot be counted on to mirror one's views, or may change his/her position after the election. This unwillingness of voters to devote the time and energy to inform themselves about issues and potential candidates is referred to as *rational ignorance*, and this tendency is reinforced by the incentive for the candidates to be vague, avoiding specifics about their views and stressing broad themes and their exemplary character for fear of alienating potential voters. While rational ignorance actually lowers the rational time and effort costs that should be expended in voting, these costs are still likely to be higher than the expected economic benefits to the voter in most cases, so that economically rational voters should not vote.

The personal costs consist of the time and effort to become informed about the candidates and going to the polls to vote. The benefits consist of the combined probability of affecting an election outcome by voting and influencing the votes of others by the voting act multiplied by the expected benefits given by the differential gains that a voter receives from one candidate over another. Comparing the much more certain costs of voting with the uncertain and meagre benefits of voting, economically rational people will choose not to vote. That is, expected costs clearly outweigh the expected benefits.

For example, suppose that on the basis of your cursory research on the views of two candidates, you determine that the election of gubernatorial Candidate X will benefit you by an additional $3000 as compared to Candidate Y. Your time and effort costs total one hour which, at the $10 an hour you would have earned if you had not spent time researching and voting, implies a $10 cost. The probability that your vote will make a difference in the election either by influencing the outcome or others' votes is usually very small, but let's assume that you are very persuasive and convince a number of your friends to vote for Candidate X. Consequently, the probability that your vote and political efforts will make a difference is say 1 in 100 000. This makes the expected benefit of voting equal to 3 cents ($3000 × 0.00001), and net benefits are –$9.97. Not voting is obviously the economically rational choice. This approach is well established, and the variables involved are, in principle, measurable. However, a great many people do vote, and in national elections sometimes the majority of the population eligible to vote do so. How does public choice theory avoid concluding that the voting population are irrational, a result that we noted does not augur well for democracy by majority vote?

The public choice theory provides important insight into why so many people do not vote, but by itself it does not explain why so many people do vote, unless they are assumed to be irrational. One way to handle this might be to use the public choice conception of voting as the central approach to voting behaviour, but to modify it by using something less restrictive than economic rationality as a guiding behavioural principle. If we drop the assumption that people are always materially driven and egoistic, we are left with a broader conception of rationality, *core rationality*. With core rationality we need only assume that voters behave consistently, which means that their basic preferences are fully formed (complete and well understood) and stable, so that choices are transitive. Transitive choices mean that if a voter prefers position A to position B, and prefers position B to position C, then she will prefer position A to position C. Were she to prefer position C to position A, we would say that her preferences are intransitive, and this would be irrational behaviour. Core rationality is a much milder requirement for behaviour and allows us to consider non-materialistic and non-egoistic (i.e. non-economic) motivations in voting behaviour. Voting may be seen as non-materialistic and altruistic, a way of carrying out one's civic duty, an obligation to others that might motivate behaviour regardless of the election outcome. In this view not only the act of voting but informing oneself about the issues is seen as a benefit, not a cost; it is the pleasure of participating in the important public process of democratic elections. This explanation conflicts with the public choice perception of a voter as a calculator of personal and material costs and benefits. We then conceive of people continually motivated by two contradictory sets of forces, with one set (economic) leading them not to vote and the other set (non-economic) leading them to vote. The percentage of people voting is the outcome of this struggle in each person's psyche. This approach does fit the general facts: that the voting percentage is never 100 per cent or zero, and some social scientists are comfortable with it (Rhoads, 1985: 153–68). However, most economists do not find this approach congenial for two reasons: economists tend to believe that in the aggregate, egoistic behaviour tends to dominate non-egoistic behaviour, which still implies non-voting as the outcome; and, even if we accept the warring motivations hypothesis, it give us no clue as to which motivational force dominates and why.

Voting may also be seen as non-materialistic and egoistic, as a social activity where the process of going to the polls and interacting with one's neighbours are the primary benefits or ways to demonstrate to one's neighbours that one is a public-spirited person, a characteristic that is often praised in a person. Each of these non-economic motivations stems from the process of voting, not the outcome of the voting process. This approach is congenial to more economists but suffers from the difficulty, even in principle, of measuring these attitudinal characteristics since they are not observable; nor do individuals have other obvious characteristics to which these effects are attached. Without the possibility of measuring these behaviours we cannot determine how pronounced they are or why. However, a more mainstream approach can be used if we see the process of voting as an instrument for another outcome than the results of the election.

We can collapse these two behaviours into a single motivation, wherein it is the desire to be perceived by others as a good citizen or person that is motivating, and voting is an inexpensive way to do this. Here, there are still separable benefits and costs to voting, but now we have an additional benefit accruing to some people: the reputation as a public-spirited citizen. Building reputational capital may have substantial material value to some people and would rationally induce some of them to engage in the voting process as part of the desire to build reputational capital at low cost. It also allows us in principle to identify some characteristics of those for whom this benefit is important by asking who would stand to gain materially from enhancing their reputation with the public. Several kinds of people immediately come to mind, including those who need to persuade members of the public about their civic concern, general reliability and dependability. Since voting is regarded as indicative of these qualities by many people (whether or not some economists believe it to be rational), rational people take this into account and make sure they are visibly engaged in the voting process or at least can say they voted. This would include potential future politicians, civic leaders, professionals such as lawyers and teachers, and salespeople. This way of perceiving the voting issue can, in principle, generate quantitative estimates of the proportion of people who will vote based on such reputational wants. This would allow us to identify those for whom the economic benefits, including reputational capital, outweigh the economic costs.

There is a final approach that assumes economic rationality of all citizens and leads to the conclusion that some, but not all, people will vote. Suppose that a rational person realizes that the immediate expected costs of voting outweigh the expected benefits of voting in terms of their personal, material well-being. Nonetheless, the *long-run rational* person may see the existence and viability of a democratic political system as preferable to other alternative political systems. If not voting is viewed as casting a vote against democracy in favour of an alternative system, then voting becomes a way to affirm support for the democratic system and the personal, material benefits this provides over non-democratic systems. If the citizen believes that there is some possibility that not voting and the public apathy that creates could help usher in an alternative system with a possible consequent loss of substantial personal, material well-being, then the calculation of benefits and costs changes significantly. Since the demise of the democratic system and the consequent meaning this would have for an individual is highly uncertain because of its uniqueness, the probabilities of the event happening and the net losses expected would vary substantially from person to person. However, it is plausible that for many people the revised expected benefits of voting may well overcome the costs of voting, so that it is economically rational for them to vote. Evidence that would tend to support this view is that in newly established democracies in which voting costs are not inordinately high, the percentage of voter turnout is much higher than it is in the USA. This would be because voters view the possibility of the dissolution of the newly established democratic system as rather high, and this is reflected in the high expected benefits of voting, given the higher probability that not voting could mean a return to a non-democratic alternative. Alternatively, the older a democracy, the lower the percentage of voter turnout can be expected in national elections. The observed existence of some voting is explained by this model, and it can also explain increased voter turnout when voters are upset with the status quo. A change in the status quo can be expected to cause a much more substantial change in personal net benefits as compared with elections, in which, regardless of which candidate wins, one is not personally and materially affected very much.

Where does this leave us? We have not fully resolved the riddle of why people vote, but we have identified some elements that can be explained when a rational economic behaviour model is employed. We have also discovered means for determining whether an expanded public choice model, modified for reputation costs, or a long-run rational model, explains and predicts reality well.

K.C.T.

REFERENCES

Browning, Edgar K. and Jacqueline M. Browning (1987), *Public Finance and the Price System*, 3rd edn, New York: Macmillan, ch. 3.

Buchanan, James M. and Gordon Tullock (1962), *The Calculus of Consent*, Ann Arbor, Michigan: The University of Michigan Press.

Downs, Anthony (1957), *An Economic Theory of Democracy*, New York: Harper & Row.

Rhoads, Steven E. (1985), *The Economist's View of the World*, New York: Cambridge University Press, ch. 9.

Tullock, Gordon (1987), 'Public Choice', in *The New Palgrave: A Dictionary of Economics*, **3**, New York: Macmillan, 1040–44.

36. The voting paradox

In 1951 Kenneth Arrow (1921–), who won a Nobel Prize in economics in 1972, showed that, with a desirable set of assumptions about human preferences, there was no voting institution, including majority voting, that could guarantee a consistent set of outcomes. In other words the basis of democracy was irrational. How can this paradox be solved?

The traditional economic solution to the inefficient market outcomes resulting from market failures has been to involve the government in the provision of goods and services. It is important then that decisions made through the democratic process have desirable characteristics. The minimum condition is consistency in the voting process, the weakest condition for rational decision making. Early on, a problem with voting had been discovered.

The voting paradox had been raised as early as 1785 by Condorcet, and dealt with more recently by Duncan Black (1948) before Arrow (1951) independently developed it in the context of welfare economics, at which point it attracted the attention of a number of economists and political scientists. Arrow's impossibility theorem showed that there was no voting system, including majority voting, that satisfied a set of conditions for an ideal voting mechanism.

First we assume that all individuals' preferences are economically rational in that they behave consistently. Given economically rational individuals, the ideal voting mechanism should satisfy the following five conditions:

1. Group rationality. The voting rule used to aggregate individual preferences should be rational in that the resulting social preferences are complete and transitive.
2. Unrestricted domain. The voting rule used should allow for all possible combinations of individual preferences.
3. Pareto optimality. The voting rule should produce a preferred choice if it is preferred by all voters.
4. Independence from non-agenda alternatives. The voting rule relating to agenda alternatives should depend only on the prefer-

ences of individuals for those alternatives and not on the evaluation of non-agenda alternatives.
5. Non-dictatorship. The voting rule should not mirror a single individual's preferences over every possible set of alternatives.

What Arrow's impossibility theorem showed was that there is no voting mechanism that can satisfy all the above ideal conditions. This can mean a number of things depending on which of the five conditions is violated. For example, if conditions 2, 3 and 4 hold, we can only achieve condition 1 if we are willing to violate condition 5 and allow a dictatorship, an objectionable conclusion for most of us! Alternatively, if we hold conditions 2, 3, 4 and 5 as essential to democracy, then condition 1 will be violated. What this means is that the voting outcome may be unstable. This inconsistency implies that the term 'in the public interest' is incoherent or without meaning when applied to a policy determined by majority vote since a different order of voting produces a different result.

Most economists have been disappointed with these results because they seemed to negate the rational use of majority voting in a democracy, raising the issue that less egalitarian forms of government might produce more rational outcomes. James Buchanan (1954), on the other hand, believes that the irrationality of majority voting is a positive and satisfying result since this implies shifting and unstable political majorities. Such majorities cannot amass power and will probably not be tyrannical.

This tendency of majority voting to produce unstable results is referred to as the voting paradox or the cyclical majority problem. Cyclical majorities occur when two issues are voted on, and the winner of one choice loses against another, and then the latter winner loses against the original loser and so forth in an endless cycle. Thus voting equilibrium is never achieved.

Consider three city council members, V1, V2, V3, and three alternative policies to choose, A, B and C. Suppose that the city council is considering three possible policies regarding a new city library: alternative A is to spend $10 million on a new library; alternative B is to spend $5 million on a new library; and alternative C is spend nothing on a new library. The council members' preferences are given in Table 36.1.

When alternative A is pitted against alternative B, B wins since council members V1 and V2 prefer it to A. When alternative B is pitted against alternative C, C wins because council members V1 and V3 prefer it to alternative A. But when alternative C is pitted against

Table 36.1   Council members' (V1,V2,V3) preference order [1]

Alternatives	V1	V2	V3
A > $10 million	3rd	2nd	1st
B > $5 million	2nd	1st	3rd
C > $0	1st	3rd	2nd

alternative A, A wins since council members V2 and V3 prefer it to C, and the cycle is endlessly repeated with no clear voting equilibrium.

The culprit in creating the cyclical majority turns out to be the way preferences are ranked. If each of the council members had, regardless of their first choice, picked their second and third choices such that they moved further away monetarily from each other, we would describe these choices as single-dimensioned or single-peaked (Black, 1948). If all voters have single-peaked preference orderings then the paradox of voting disappears. However, this condition negates Arrow's condition 2 because single-peakedness puts a restriction on the preference orderings of individuals. Single-peaked preferences for all voters would seem to be uncommon because they require that the choice among alternatives depend on a simple and common dimension among voters. In this example, council member V3 may reasonably say that he supports building a high-quality library for educational reasons (A), but if we do not build a high-quality library, he would rather not build a low-quality library because this is less emotionally satisfying to him than no library (C). Two different dimensions, educational quality and emotional satisfaction, play a dominant role in different alternatives. Another possibility is that both conditions 2 and 4 may be violated. Here council member V3 prefers a high-quality library or none at all because the $5 million could in the future be spent on other, and currently non-agenda, projects that V3 feels are more effective in meeting community needs than a $5 million library. So double-peakedness would seem to be a normal characteristic of some voters' preferences on issues. On the other hand, single-peakedness may be more common when choosing among candidates for office.

While politicians sometimes espouse a number of views on various issues, they often attempt to shape the voter perception of their views along a single spectrum of 'liberal' and 'conservative' ideology (Downs, 1957). That these ideological terms tend to change meaning over time is less important than whether, at any point in time, they provide a commonly understood and single dimension with which to evaluate political candidates. Why would political candidates try to create a simplified understanding of their views?

A public choice approach would argue that politicians understand that the time and effort cost for voters to become informed are higher than the differential benefits of the favoured candidate and so potential voters will not vote – the voting behaviour puzzle. Creating a one-dimensional ideological persona is a way to reduce voter costs of being uninformed and increase the differential benefits perceived by their candidacy. An alternative, but not necessarily inconsistent, view is that the shaping of voter preference along a single ideological dimension creates single-peakedness and thus predictability of how a candidate is performing and how their strategy needs to evolve over the course of the campaign. Leading candidates would be expected to adopt this strategy while dark-horse candidates would be expected to stress either multiple issues or a single issue that cannot be easily subsumed under the current 'liberal' and 'conservative' labels. In effect dark-horse candidates are attempting to create double-peaked preferences among the voters because they have nothing to gain by voters perceiving candidates along a single ideological dimension that would seal their loss in the election. The real-world behaviour of both front-running and dark-horse candidates is consistent with this hypothesis.

Double-peaked preferences are a necessary but not a sufficient condition for the voting paradox to occur. For example, if council member V1's choices are ranked CAB, then we can see by examining Table 36.2 that A wins unambiguously. That is, no voting paradox occurs despite council member V3's double-peaked preferences.

Table 36.2   Council members' (V1,V2,V3) preference order [2]

Alternatives	V1	V2	V3
A > $10 million	2nd	2nd	1st
B > $5 million	3rd	1st	3rd
C > $0	1st	3rd	2nd

The key difference between the two sets of city council preferences is that in Table 36.1 each council member's preference is completely different, with no agreement as to rank on each of the three alternatives considered, while in Table 36.2 council members V1 and V2 agree on the ranking of alternative A. As the number of voters increases for a given set of alternatives, the likelihood that they will disagree on the rankings decreases and the probability of a voting paradox declines if we assume that each preference ordering is equally likely. Thus where the number of voters on an issue is large, double-peakedness seems less likely to create a real-world voting paradox problem despite the fact that Arrow demonstrated that it can never be logically ruled out.

Voting paradoxes are also less likely because real-world voting institutions do not fit the model of voting conditions Arrow proposed. In the real world of voting, strategic manipulation of one's vote can increase the power of the vote to effect the results desired. Manipulation strategies may increase the efficiency of the voting process by accounting for intensity of individual preferences, and they invariably overcome the irrationality inherent in voting systems revealed by Arrow's impossibility theorem. Furthermore, additional consideration of the theory of voting led to the Gibbard–Satterthwaite theorem that strategic manipulation is endemic to all voting systems except a dictatorial one (Schotter, 1994: 557). One common type of strategic manipulation is log-rolling, or vote trading.

Log-rolling occurs when a politician votes for an issue he would have opposed in exchange for another politician's vote on an issue he supports more than the one he opposes. This institution allows voters to register intensity of preference, a real-world interest not included in Arrow's ideal conditions. Log-rolling negates the paradox of voting and generates a consistent social outcome – condition 1, by violating condition 4 – independence from non-agenda alternatives. In our library example represented by Table 36.2, V2's first preference, alternative B, cannot win. Suppose, however, that V2 tells V1 that if V1 will vote for alternative B, then V2 will vote for V1's preferred choice on the next issue. If V1 knows that on the next issue his preferred choice is not likely to win, then it may be in his interest to trade his vote on alternative B now for V2's support on the next issue. Log-rolling is common in democratic voting systems, including the US Congress.

Another type of strategic manipulation is agenda control. Agenda control is a way societies avoid the cyclical majority by not letting the cycle of votes be completed to reveal the intransitivity of the process. Agenda manipulation, which violates condition 1, group rationality, accomplishes this. It occurs when a political leader is able to control the order in which alternatives are voted on. Agenda manipulation increases the likelihood of the preferred outcome by controlling the process of voting on alternatives. In our library example from Table 36.1, suppose the chairperson of the city council is V1, who controls the order of voting on the three alternatives by pairs, and knows how the other members will vote. In order to have his preferred choice win, he will first put alternative A against alternative B and alternative B will win. Then alternative B will be pitted against alternative C whereupon alternative C, his preferred choice, will win. Were he to have put alternative C up against alternative A in the first round, alternative A would have won, and alternative B would have won when pitted against alternative A.

Another strategic manipulation institution that allows for the expression of intensity of preference is strategic voting, wherein a voter votes for something other than her first choice because she believes it has no chance of winning and wishes to prevent another choice from being selected. That is, there may be an incentive not to let one's vote reflect one's true preferences. Like log-rolling, strategic voting allows what would be a losing first-preference win by voting in such a way that the winning choice under non-strategic voting does not make it to the last round of voting. For example, if in the previous example V1 controls the agenda order, this implies that alternative C will win as long as all three council members vote their true preferences. Suppose, however, that V2 dislikes alternative C intensely, and his primary goal is to make sure it does not win. Then in the first round, when V1 puts alternative A against alternative B, V2 will lie and vote for A, allowing A to win the first round. In the second round, when alternative A is pitted against alternative B, A will win. While A was only V2's second choice, this outcome is preferable, given V2's intensity of preference against alternative C.

There is a final reason that the voting paradox may not be as serious for democracy as it seems to be from Arrow's impossibility theorem. Individuals in the Arrow model are assumed to be economically rational, and this means that their underlying preferences are fully formed, unchanging and complete. However, voters often face issues whose costs and benefits are difficult to discern and for which their preferences may not be well developed. If this is the case then the voting paradox loses its importance because its startling conclusion of social inconsistency of voting outcomes becomes a secondary problem. With individual political preferences that are not fully formed, changing and incomplete, the primary task of the politicians from a system perspective becomes to engage the citizenry in a dialogue to reveal and evolve political preferences, and the primary political problem becomes finding a specific political process that enables this continual political discussion to take place (Habermas, 1979: 186). Voting becomes the practical way to solve disputes left unresolved after discussion takes place. Most economists have not found this approach congenial.

K.C.T.

REFERENCES

Arrow, Kenneth J. (1951), *Social Choice and Individual Values*, New York: John Wiley.

Black, Duncan (1948), 'On the Rationale of Group Decision-Making', *Journal of Political Economy*, **56**, 23–34.

Buchanan, James (1954), 'Social Choice, Democracy, and Free Markets', *Journal of Political Economy*, **62**, 114–23.

Downs, Anthony (1957), *An Economic Theory of Democracy*, New York: Harper & Row.

Habermas, Juergen (1979), *Communication and Evolution of Society*, translated by T. McCarthy, Boston, Massachusetts: Beacon Press.

Schotter, Andrew (1994), *Microeconomics – A Modern Approach*, New York: HarperCollins, ch. 18.

37.   A taxing debate

Argument A: *'To reduce the federal deficit, taxes should be raised. An increase in taxes will cut the deficit, reduce interest rates and stimulate the economy.'*
Argument B: *'To reduce the federal deficit, taxes should be cut. A tax cut will stimulate economic activity, expand the tax base, and increase government revenues, which will reduce the deficit.'*
Which argument should prevail?

For many economists, the answer depends to a large degree on where we are on the Laffer curve. The Laffer curve is a theoretical construct showing the relationship between the rate of taxation and the level of government revenues, as in Figure 37.1. It was invented by economist

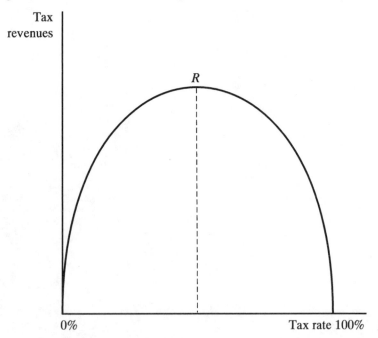

Figure 37.1   The Laffer curve

182

Arthur Laffer. On the vertical axis are annual tax revenues. On the horizontal axis are tax rates from 0 to 100 per cent. Theoretically, there is an 'ideal' tax rate that will generate a maximum level of taxes collected (R). In the figure, tax revenues are maximized at a specified marginal tax rate, but empirically no one knows for sure what is the most efficient rate. The only conclusion most economists agree on is that tax rates can become too onerous at some point and reduce revenues rather than raise them, but no one agrees on what that rate is.

Let us first discuss Argument B, the supply-side case for cutting marginal tax rates. Supply-siders argue that the actual tax rate is to the right of R in Figure 37.1. Therefore, tax cuts increase incentives for working, saving and investing, and therefore increase the job base and productivity. These incentives, in turn, expand the tax base and increase taxes collected.

Can tax cutting increase government revenues? There are several historical cases to look at, for example, the Kennedy–Johnson tax cuts, 1963–65, and the Reagan tax cuts, 1981–88. In both cases, the marginal tax rates were lowered, and in both cases, government tax revenues rose and, in particular, wealthier citizens paid more in taxes than in the previous period. In 1963–65, the top 5 per cent income-earners paid 7.7 per cent more in taxes and in 1981–88, the top 5 per cent paid 44.0 per cent more in taxes (Miller, 1994: 265).

Critics, however, point out that marginal tax rates fell at a time when other things were not held equal. For example, fiscal and monetary policies were both expansionary during this time, which would normally stimulate economic activity and raise tax revenues anyway. In addition, tax cuts helped the rich more than the poor and middle class. In short, the benefits of supply-side tax cuts have been exaggerated (Baumol and Blinder, 1994: 705–8).

What about Argument A? Keynesians argue that the actual tax rate may be to the left of point R in Figure 37.1. Marginal tax rates were raised in the 1990s under Presidents Bush and Clinton, and indeed, tax revenues increased, the official deficit declined, and interest rates dropped. But, again, not all things were held equal. Following the 1990–91 recession, monetary policy was expansionary, pushing interest rates down and spurring an economic recovery. This alone could have increased revenues. Moreover, the US economy, like the rest of the world, has moved toward a more global, free-market economy, with lower tariff and quota barriers, thus stimulating a worldwide economic boom. Under these circumstances, it is difficult to pinpoint the effect of tax changes.

Finally, there is the problem of budget financing itself. Taxation is only one half of the budget accounting statement. A tax increase does not necessarily translate into a budget deficit reduction. It could encourage Congress to spend more on their favourite programmes. The reality is that over the past 50 years, tax revenues and expenditures have moved together – both upward. In short, there is no guarantee that a tax increase will reduce the deficit.

M.S.

REFERENCES

Baumol, William J. and Alan S. Blinder (1994), *Economics: Principles and Policies*, 6th edn, New York: Dryden Press.
Miller, Roger LeRoy (1994), *Economics Today*, 8th edn, New York: HarperCollins.

38. The blessings of destruction

Frédéric Bastiat (1801–50) considers the case of a young hoodlum who throws a brick through a window of a baker's shop. This act of violence creates business to replace the window. Therefore, is not the hoodlum a public benefactor rather than a menace to society?

Bastiat's essay, 'What is Seen and What is Not Seen', was, to some extent, a response to the satirical allegory of Bernard Mandeville, *The Fable of the Bees*, in which Mandeville claimed that private vices were public virtues. In his poem, Mandeville suggested that a community engaged in extravagant living and other 'vicious propensities' would enjoy immense prosperity, while a society converted to parsimonious living, debt reduction, disarmament, and 'honest' sobriety would suffer a painful economic depression. In sum, 'Bare Virtue can't make Nations live in Splendour' (Mandeville, 1924).

To respond to Mandeville's clever paradox, Bastiat used the example of a young hoodlum who destroys a glass window in a baker's shop (Bastiat, 1964). The community is shocked by this act of violence, but upon reflection, suggests that the baker's misfortune has its bright side. It will create business for the glassmaker. Moreover, the money received by the glassmaker will be used to buy other things from other merchants. And so the broken window provides money and employment in ever-widening circles. The logical conclusion is that, far from being a criminal, the young hoodlum was a public benefactor. Instead of being sent to jail, he should be given an award.

Bastiat then questions this optimistic conclusion by focusing on the other side of the story. The shopkeeper has lost some money because he had to pay for an unexpected expense, a new window. Perhaps he was going to buy a suit, but now his order is cancelled – the suit won't be made. The glassmaker's gain of business is merely the tailor's loss of business. From a community viewpoint, the community may have a new window, but it has lost an old window and a new suit. On net balance, the community is no better off. In sum, the young hoodlum remains a public menace.

Bastiat concludes, 'There is only one difference between a bad economist and a good one: the bad economist confines himself to the visible effect; the good economist takes into account both the effect that can be seen and those effects that must be foreseen' (Bastiat, 1964). Henry Hazlitt, who used the Bastiat story as the one 'lesson' in economics, states, 'The art of economics consists in looking not merely at the immediate but at the longer effects of any act or policy; it consists in tracing the consequences of that policy for one group but for all groups' (Hazlitt, 1979: 17).

The controversy over Mandeville's paradox is debated even today. Are war and natural disasters good for the economy? The alleged blessings of destruction are frequently promoted in academia and the media. Economic commentators have argued that wars, earthquakes, and defence spending can benefit the economy. Recently economic historian Michael Bernstein argued that 'the enormous expenditures on public goods during the various cold-war (and hot-war) offensives of the 50's and 60's were, among other things, responsible for America's postwar economic success' ('Letters', *New York Times Book Review*, 12 May 1996). Following the devastating earthquake in Kobe, Japan, in January 1995, Nicholas D. Kristof wrote, 'some experts said that in some ways the earthquake could give a boost to an economy struggling to recover from a long recession' (*New York Times*, 18 January 1995). Even Keynes suggested that, during a depression, ' "To dig holes in the ground", paid for out of savings, will increase, not only employment, but the real national dividend of useful goods and services' (Keynes, 1936: 220). Keynes, incidentally, spoke kindly of Mandeville's parable (Keynes, 1936: 359–62).

IS WAR GOOD FOR THE ECONOMY?

World War II has been used to support the thesis that war is good for the economy. In the USA, GDP more than doubled from 1940 to 1945, real income rose and unemployment virtually disappeared (Robertson, 1973: 709). Some experts claim that the high rates of economic growth in postwar Japan and Germany were due, in part, to their need completely to rebuild their cities.

Recently, however, some economists have revised their views on World War II (Higgs, 1992; Vedder and Galloway, 1991). They conclude that on net balance people's standards of living declined as measured by per capita real consumption during the war and recovered following the war. Historian Robert Higgs states:

This belief [that war is good for the economy] is ill-founded, because it does not recognize that the United States had a command economy during the war. From 1942 to 1946 some macroeconomic performance measures were statistically inaccurate; others are conceptually inappropriate. A better grounded interpretation is that during the war the economy was a huge arsenal in which the well-being of consumers deteriorated. After the war genuine prosperity returned for the first time since 1929. (Higgs, 1992: 41)

In short, war brings tradeoffs and restructuring. In the case of World War II, the benefits included higher industrial output, employment and income, and advances in medical and other technology; the drawbacks included inflation, shortages of basic consumer products, rationing, postponement of education and business opportunities, mass destruction of property, and last but not least, human casualties and loss of life.

In conclusion, in measuring the effects of economic behaviour, it is necessary to examine all effects, benefits and costs, short-term and long-term, micro and macro.

M.S.

REFERENCES

Bastiat, Frédéric (1964 [1844]), *Economic Sophisms*, New York: D. Van Nostrand.

Hazlitt, Henry (1979), *Economics in One Lesson*, 2nd edn, New York: Arlington House.

Higgs, Robert (1992), 'Wartime Prosperity? A Reassessment of the U.S. Economy in the 1940s', *Journal of Economic History*, **52** (1), 41–60.

Keynes, John Maynard (1936), *The General Theory of Employment, Interest and Money*, New York: Macmillan.

Mandeville, Bernard (1924 [1714]), *The Fable of the Bees*, edited by F.B. Kaye. London: Oxford University Press.

Robertson, Ross M. (1973), *History of the American Economy*, 3rd edn, New York: Harcourt Brace Jovanovich.

Vedder, Richard K. and Lowell Galloway (1991), 'The Great Depression of 1946', *Review of Austrian Economics*, **5** (2), 3–31.

39.   The interest rate dilemma

Argument A: *'Higher interest rates are good for the economy because it means higher income for retirees invested in money market funds and Treasury bills. This additional income will stimulate the economy.'*
Argument B: *'Higher interest rates are bad for the economy because it means borrowing money is more expensive and will therefore hurt business and consumer spending.'*
Which argument is correct? Are higher interest rates good or bad for the economy?

In a dynamic economy, issues like the above come up frequently. Rising farm prices are good for the farmers, but bad for shoppers at the grocery store. A declining dollar is good for exporters, but bad for importers. And rising interest rates are good for income-seekers and retirees, but bad for individual and commercial borrowers.

On balance which is better for the economy? During the early 1980s, interest rates skyrocketed, with the prime rate rising to 21 per cent. National leaders decried this credit crunch, but many investors were delighted to earn double-digit returns on money market funds and Treasury bills. These investors expressed sadness when the interest rates declined to single-digit levels by the late 1980s.

The issue comes down to this: which effect had the greatest impact on the economy, higher interest rates on investors' income, or higher interest rates on business activity? Most economists would agree that business activity is of far greater importance than investment income and hence, on a net balance, higher interest rates are bad for the economy. The net effect was a recession in the early 1980s. Real GDP declined.

It should also be pointed out that not all income-seekers benefited from rising interest rates during the early 1980s. Holders of long-term corporate and government bonds saw their investments lose considerable value during this time. Stock prices typically fall when real interest rates rise. Only those who held short-term money market instruments (money market funds and Treasury bills) and those who locked in high yields on bank certificates of deposit at the height of the credit crunch benefited from rising rates. Investors in general and retirees in particular usually hold a much larger share of their portfolio in stocks and bonds rather than certificates of deposit and short-term money market instruments. In sum, higher interest rates are not only bad for business, but bad for most investors and retirees.

M.S.

40.   The population puzzler

If a married couple has two children, the chance of having a boy and a girl is 50 per cent. If they have four children, the chance of having two boys and two girls is ... only 37.5 per cent (six out of 16 possibilities). If they have eight kids, the chance of having four boys and four girls is 27.3 per cent. In other words, as the world is populated more and more, there is less and less chance of having an equal number of boys and girls. Yet historically large populations are approximately 50–50 male–female. How do you reconcile this contradiction?

To determine the chances that a couple will have an equal number of boys and girls, the general binominal formulation is as follows:

$$P_r(x) = \binom{n}{x} p^x q^{n-x} \; ; 0 < p < 1, \, q = 1-p, \, x = 0,1,2,...,n$$

$$\binom{n}{x} = \frac{n!}{x!(n-x)!}$$

For n, an even number, and $x = n/2$ and $p = q = 1/2$, we get:

$$Pr\left(\frac{n}{2}\right) = \frac{n!}{\left(\frac{n}{2}\right)! \left(\frac{n}{2}\right)!} \left(\frac{1}{2}\right)^n$$

Sample values are as follows:

Number of children (n)	Predicted chances of equal boys and girls
2	0.50
4	0.3750
8	0.27343750
16	0.196380615
32	0.139949934
64	0.099346754
128	0.070386092

.
.
.

Notice that as $n\to\infty$, $P\,(n/2)\to 0$.

Figure 40.1 illustrates the relationship between the number of children and the probability of having equal numbers. The figure also clarifies the population puzzler. It is true that the chances of having an exactly equal number of boys and girls declines as the number of children increases. But you will also note that as the number of offspring increases, the distribution of the sample approaches a normal bell-shaped curve. Thus, as the height of the distribution declines, the concentration increases. In essence, the greater concentration means that the proportion of the population near one-half increases. Thus the chances of having an exact number of boys and girls declines, but the chances of a large population having approximately equal

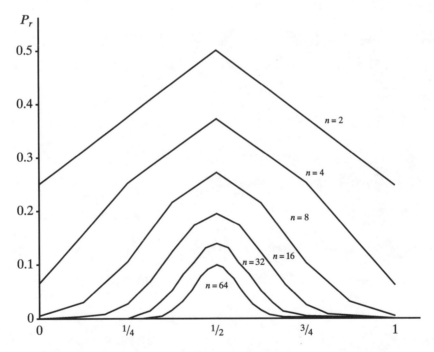

Figure 40.1   Probabilities of having equal numbers of male and female offspring

numbers of boys and girls increases! Thus the population puzzler is resolved. (Thanks to Royal Skousen for providing the statistical work.)

M.S.

41. The efficiency versus equality puzzle

The economic virtue of the market system resides in its ability to produce more than a non-market system of what people want in a society. Yet there is no guarantee that everyone will participate in the overall benefit to society of a market system. Indeed, the USA, the most market-oriented industrial country in the world, also has one of the most unequal income distributions of any of the industrial countries. Does more efficient production invariably imply more unequally distributed income?

The equality versus efficiency puzzle is one of the most important in economics. Confusion begins immediately if we do not define what we mean by the two terms at issue. Let's start with equality. Equality refers to equality of income or consumption or wealth distribution, all of which measure material well-being. Arthur Okun (1929–79) argued that 'any insistence on carving the pie into equal slices would shrink the size of the pie. That fact poses the trade-off between economic equality and economic efficiency' (Okun, 1975: 48). Thus if the tradeoff exists, then to argue for more efficiency in an economy appears tantamount to arguing for more inequality.

Efficiency can have a variety of meanings, but economic efficiency means that given a society's resources and technologies, a society is producing as much output as it can that satisfies people's desires for that output. Both production (supply) and desire for that production (demand) are simultaneously taken into account in economic efficiency. If, in a society, one person could be better off without someone else being made worse off, an action that would make that person better off is said to be an efficient action. The act of voluntary exchange is inherently efficient since the participants in these transactions engage in them to make themselves mutually better off. Societal efficiency is achieved when no production changes or further exchanges take place, a position referred to as Pareto optimality from the economist Vilfredo Pareto (1848–1923). Of course, this is a hypothetical position in a static world. In the real dynamic world, production and exchange are always ongoing, and efficiency is always in process.

These acts of production and exchange generate greater resources for the people involved. Since most people receive income from wages and salaries and fringe benefits, and over 70 per cent of national income in the USA is generated by these, growing income depends on the way that wages and salaries grow. Wages and salaries depend on worker productivity, that is, their efficiency. As efficiency increases, incomes increase, and per capita measures of societal well-being can be expected to reflect this. Thus efficient production and exchange are associated with a higher level of material well-being for most if not all members of society. Consequently, we can use GNP per capita to approximate the average material well-being of a country. Then we can compare countries in terms of their GNP per capita and income distribution to suggest whether or not there is an efficiency/equality tradeoff.

Distribution can be measured in a variety of ways, but a common measure is the percentage of consumption or income gained by a given percentage of the population, such as each quintile, or 20 per cent of the population. Perfect equality would be 20 per cent of the population with 20 per cent of the income, 40 per cent of the population with 40 per cent of the income and so forth, so that everyone earns the same income. Perfect inequality would be 99.9 . . . per cent of the population with no income and one person with all of the income.

Although income and consumption distribution data are collected for different countries, there are enough differences in the way they are calculated that important problems of comparability remain. We must use the data with great caution to render them useful (World Bank, 1995: 220–21). No country in the world has anything approaching equal consumption or income or wealth distribution. Income distribution is more dispersed among low-income countries than among high-income or industrial countries such as the USA. Countries with the most unequal distributions of income are those where the lowest 40 per cent of the population has less than 10 per cent of the income or consumption and the highest 20 per cent has over 60 per cent of the income or consumption. None of these are high-income economies and include low-income countries such as Tanzania, Honduras, and Lesotho; middle-income countries of Guatemala and Brazil; and the upper middle-income country of South Africa. The countries with the most equal income or consumption distribution come from all income strata and include those where the lowest 40 per cent of the population has at least 20 per cent of the income or consumption and the highest 20 per cent of the population has less than 40 per cent of the income or consumption. Countries in this group include the low-income countries of Nepal and Pakistan; the middle-income countries of Bulgaria and

Poland; the upper middle-income country of Hungary, and the higher-income or industrial countries of Spain, the Netherlands, Belgium, Sweden and Japan. The USA has the highest per capita GNP of any country in the world, yet the lowest 40 per cent of the population had less than 16 per cent of the income in 1985, a figure that exceeded only that in Australia, the United Kingdom and Singapore, among 20 industrial countries. In the USA the highest 20 per cent of the population has almost 42 per cent of the income, a figure exceeded in the industrial world only by New Zealand, Australia, Hong Kong, the United Kingdom, Singapore and Switzerland.

What is clear from our brief survey is that countries at a higher level of economic development tend to have income distributions that are not among the most unequal and may have income distributions that are among the most equal. Evidently efficiency (greater GNP per capita) and equality (more equal income distribution) are not necessarily inversely related across all levels of development. Moreover, high-income countries tend to have more market-oriented economic systems than countries with a lower GNP per capita, as tradition and government involvement is stronger in the latter. However, the two countries that have the highest per capita income, the USA and Switzerland, also have two of the most unequal income distributions among the industrial countries. Also, the countries not in the lowest income group that are among those with the most equal income distributions are all countries that are either market socialist or have heavy government involvement in the economy. So while a strong market orientation does seem to be a prerequisite for greater material well-being, more government involvement seems a feature in more equal income distribution for higher-income countries. Differing social and cultural values may help explain this.

The efficiency versus equality puzzle for high-income countries is really about the tradeoff between two different conceptions of equality. Efficiency-oriented market economies emphasize and value equality of opportunity for economic agents such as workers, consumers and firms within the context of less constrained markets. If people differ in terms of the wage and salary that their skills fetch in the market, then emphasis on equality of opportunity guarantees that a society will have more inequality of outcomes. Socially oriented market economies place more emphasis and value on equality of outcomes in terms of income distribution for workers and firms and the pursuit of social programmes to achieve income equality. If people believe their differential skills are not being adequately rewarded, work effort tends to lessen and so will efficiency.

At the individual level, the equality of opportunity versus the equality of outcomes tradeoff reflects a difference in beliefs about what motivates people in their economic lives. More purely market-oriented systems rest on the assumption that people are most materially motivated by absolute levels of increase in their standard of living. More socially oriented market systems assume that people are most materially motivated by relative levels of their standard of living.

For example, suppose that everyone in the office works a 40-hour week and is given a choice by the manager: next year's rise will be 4 per cent for everyone who will all do the same kind of work, or 8 per cent for two people whose extra productivity will be put to work more effectively and 6 per cent for everyone else. In a pure market-oriented economic system where equality of opportunity is the dominant social value, all people will select the 6 per cent rise because it is higher and seen as fairer even though their position worsens relative to the two people who earn 8 per cent. In a pure socially oriented economic system where equality of outcome is the dominant social value all people will select the 4 per cent rise and see it as fairer because their position will not get worse relative to anyone else's. These differences in motivation become more important the greater the differences in the market values of workers in a society.

For great differences in material well-being among countries, there is evidently no tradeoff between equality and efficiency, as greater efficiency leads to higher per capita income and greater equality in income distribution – up to a point. For high-income countries the tradeoff exists but should now be less puzzling. Because all high-income economies are market-oriented systems characterized by workers of varying skills, equality of opportunity is important and wages and salaries will differ. But all high-income countries also place some value on equality of outcome, as revealed by the existence of social welfare systems that create a safety net in all these countries. The USA does have the highest per capita income among the industrial countries, and it also has one of the least generous social welfare systems. By valuing efficiency relatively more than other industrial countries, the USA has opted for a more unequal income distribution than those countries. In high-income market-oriented economic systems where the market invariably values skills differentially, individuals over time choose between absolute and relative income concerns. This slowly evolving societal choice will be reflected in the creation of private and public institutions that emphasize a mix of equality of opportunity and equality of outcome. The efficiency versus equality puzzle can be understood, but the tradeoff always remains.

K.C.T.

REFERENCES

Okun, Arthur (1975), *Equality and Efficiency: The Big Tradeoff*, Washington: Brookings Institution.

US Department of Commerce (1995), *Survey of Current Business*, Washington, D.C.

World Bank (1995), *World Development Report 1995*, New York: Oxford University Press, esp. Table 30, 'Income Distribution and PPP estimates of GNP'.

42. The national debt: asset or liability?

Economist Robert Eisner states, 'The greater a person's debt, given his assets, the less his net worth; the greater the Government's debt, the greater the people's net worth' (Eisner, New York Times, 19 March 1994). How is this possible?

Professor Eisner made this statement in an editorial defending the national debt and deficit spending. His ambiguity is technically possible by emphasizing micro over macro. From an individual (micro) viewpoint, borrowing money does *ipso facto* reduce one's net worth. A private debt is a liability to the borrower. But by the same token it is an asset to the lender.

Now let's look at the national debt held by the US Treasury. From an investor's viewpoint, the national debt can be viewed as an asset. It consists of Treasury securities of all kinds – bonds, notes, bills and US savings bonds – held by individuals, banks, brokerage houses and other financial institutions.

But Eisner ignores several salient factors in the national debt equation. First, he ignores the liability side of the ledger. From the borrower's viewpoint – the federal government's – the national debt is a liability. It is a financial obligation in the future. Moreover, further deficit spending may reduce the net worth of the US government, assuming no change in the government's capital assets (buildings, land, etc.).

It is possible, of course, that the government's assets may rise and thereby offset the deficit if the government uses the proceeds of the bond issue to build or purchase capital goods. As Gregory Mankiw states, 'under capital budgeting, government borrowing to finance the purchase of a capital good would not raise the deficit' (Mankiw, 1992: 432). Naturally, the value of these capital assets is a major issue. Some assets may be valuable, others may be wasted. Mankiw asks,

> For example, should the interstate highway system be counted as an asset of the government? If so, what is its value? What about the stockpile of nuclear weapons? Should spending on education be treated as expenditure

on human capital? These difficult questions must be answered if the government is to adopt a capital budget. (Mankiw, 1942: 432)

Another issue is the value of the Treasury securities themselves. The people's assets – the investors' Treasury securities – do not necessarily increase in value when the government increases the national debt. Eisner assumes that the price of government securities stays the same. That may not be the case. If interest rates stay the same or decline, Eisner is correct. The value of the 'people's assets' will rise, at least from the investor's viewpoint. But we must not forget the possibility that private investment (also the 'people's assets') may decline and offset the rise in government investment ('crowding out').

But what if the government runs too heavy a deficit and pushes interest rates higher? Then Treasury security prices will move lower. As a result, the value of the 'people's assets' will fall, sometimes dramatically. Historically, there are many cases of collapsing government bond prices, both in the United States and abroad (Malabre, 1987). In cases of excessive government red ink and runaway inflation, the government bond market has completely disappeared ('no bid'), at least in its local currency. In short, there are severe limitations surrounding Eisner's optimistic view that government bonds are an asset and not a liability.

M.S.

REFERENCES

Eisner, Robert (1994), 'Off Balance', *New York Times*, 19 March.
Malabre, Alfred (1987), *Beyond Our Means*, New York: Random House.
Mankiw, N. Gregory (1992), *Macroeconomics*, 2nd edn, New York: Worth Publishers.

43.   The Leontief paradox

The Heckscher–Ohlin or factor proportions theory, the dominant approach to comparative advantage in international trade, says that a country will specialize in and export those goods using its most abundant factor most intensively. In the 1950s it was clear that the USA was more capital-abundant than any other country. Yet when Wassily Leontief looked at the evidence, he found that the USA was exporting labour-intensive goods. How is this possible?

In 1953 Wassily Leontief (1906–), the inventor of input–output analysis and future Nobel laureate, published an empirical study of US trade to test the Heckscher–Ohlin model (Leontief, 1956). He looked at US capital and labour requirements to produce $1 million in exports and $1 million in US goods that directly competed with imports – as a proxy for relevant US imports. He had fully expected to find that the USA exported capital-intensive goods, and that US import-competing goods were labour-intensive, as predicted by the Heckscher–Ohlin model, since observers agreed that the USA was the world's most capital-abundant country. However, he found that the USA was exporting labour-intensive goods and US-importing competing goods were capital-intensive with an import to export capital labour ratio of 1.3 (Appleyard and Field, 1995: 148).

One conclusion that might have been drawn from Leontief's evidence is that the Heckscher–Ohlin, or H–O, theory of international trade (Heckscher, 1949; Ohlin, 1933) is simply wrong. Such a conclusion has been rejected by most academic economists who dealt with the issue, including Leontief. This was for two reasons, one historic and one more immediate. First, H–O theory represented a further development of the principle of comparative advantage associated with David Ricardo (1772–1823): countries will specialize in and export the products in which they have the lowest relative costs. The principle of comparative advantage is deeply embedded in economic theory. It had been the primary theoretical basis for economists' understanding of international trade for the previous 150 years, and would not be rejected on the basis of one negative empirical result, albeit a significant one. Second, H–O theory was also theoretically attractive because its structure is such that it could be used to give substance and impetus to the development of general equilibrium theory which was being more rigorously developed in the early 1950s by Paul Samuelson (DeMarchi, 1976; 112–13). Thus H–O theory itself generated or was closely related to additional theoretical results that form an important part of the development of general equilibrium theory. The Rybczyanski theorem shows that an increase in the supply of one productive factor in a country, say labour, increases the output of the labour-intensive good and reduces the output of the capital-intensive good. The Stolper–Samuelson theorem shows that trade increases the real incomes of capital owners in the capital-scarce country and reduces the real incomes of capital owners in the capital-abundant country. The factor-price equalization theorem extends the Stolper–Samuelson logic and shows that in the absence of trade restrictions and transport costs, trade equalizes factor prices. And once general equilibrium theory had been developed by 1960 and had become the core theoretical basis for mainstream economics, any outright rejection of H–O theory would cast strong doubt on the general equilibrium theory which had evolved from it. Moreover, mainstream economics is theory-driven, not empirically driven, and so rejection of economic theory from empirical evidence would only be made after all other possibilities had been exhausted.

Most research directed to solving the Leontief paradox focused on the restrictive assumptions of H–O theory or on the empirical specification of the model and the data used to test it. H–O theory assumes that there are no trade barriers or, alternatively, the trade barriers that do exist do not distort factor intensity in production. The US tariff structure tends to protect industries using large quantities of unskilled labour. Since the actual composition of US imports was used to weight import-competing production, this tends to bias import-competing production toward more capital intensity than would exist were there a factor-neutral tariff structure, or none at all. This provides a partial explanation of the Leontief paradox, but allowing for such tariff biases does not eliminate it.

Another potential explanation is factor-intensity reversals. H–O theory assumes that a good always has a dominant factor intensity regardless of relative factor prices. If agricultural products were capital-intensive in the USA, but the reverse were true in other countries, this would be a factor-intensity reversal. Factor intensity could not be unambiguously identified for agricultural goods. If the USA imports agricultural products it is measured as capital-intensive since that is the factor intensity of the product in the USA. Although there is some evidence for factor reversals, they may not resolve the Leontief paradox if other omitted productive factors are accounted for (Appleyard and Field, 1995: 135, 151–2).

Another possible explanation is demand reversals. H–O theory assumes that tastes are identical between trading countries. Demand reversals occur when a country has a strong preference for a good using its abundant factor most intensively. If the USA, the capital-abundant country, has strong preference for capital-intensive autos relative to labour-intensive clothes, the rent/wage ratio may be driven up so much that it becomes higher than in its trading partners. In this case the USA would have a comparative advantage in the production of clothes, exporting them to other countries for automobiles. Other, labour-abundant countries, would have a comparative advantage in auto production and export them to the USA. This is the opposite trade pattern from that predicted by H–O theory. While this theoretical possibility exists, there is no evidence that it is empirically important in world trade. Demand conditions are similar in the industrial countries that comprise the bulk of world trade (Ethier, 1995: 156).

Another potential resolution of the paradox centred on the fact that natural resources, like human capital, are excluded from H–O theory, which assumes only two productive factors. It turns out that many import-competing industries in the USA are very resource-intensive, and such industries, like minerals and forest products, also tend to use a great deal of physical capital to convert them into useful products. If natural resource industries are separated out from the rest of the data, US exports become more capital-intensive than US import-competing products (Appleyard and Field, 1995: 152). So what Leontief's study may have picked up was that US imports were natural-resource-intensive, for which physical capital serves as a complementary input and a partial proxy in the empirical study.

H–O theory specifies only two productive factors, capital and labour. Leontief himself offered the view that the results he obtained might be due to the inadequacy of the data that failed to capture the productive superiority of US workers relative to foreign workers, a superiority due to better US entrepreneurship that organized workers more efficiently. This explanation did not convincingly explain why US labour was more productive than foreign labour because the entrepreneurship argument would seem to apply equally to capital as to labour. If, instead, labour is separated into skilled and unskilled categories, and Leontief's results are re-examined using human capital per worker along with physical capital per worker, labour and natural resource, US exports are revealed to be more skilled-labour-intensive than US import-competing products (Appleyard and Field, 1995: 154–6). The Leontief paradox can be resolved by reinterpreting the most abundant US factor as human capital and not raw labour. US exports were more human-capital-intensive than US import-competing products. Nonetheless, acceptance of this result again moves us away from the H–O theory because more than two productive factors are needed to explain trade patterns.

While the inclusion of natural resources and human capital, along with tariffs, may help resolve the Leontief paradox, they also complicate the H–O theory which generated it. Once we increase the number of countries, commodities, and factors of production beyond two each, to mirror reality more closely, H–O conclusions about factor abundance and factor intensity become more complex and less powerful. Alternative theories of international trade patterns have been developed that loosen the assumptions of H–O theory and help further resolve the Leontief paradox.

These theories include the human skills theory (Ethier, 1995: 159), the technology lag theory (Appleyard and Field, 1995: 163–4), product cycle theory (Appleyard and Field, 1995: 164–8), internal demand theory (Ethier, 1995: 161–2) and new trade theory (Krugman, 1994: 226–44) among others. Taken together these alternatives to H–O theory have assumed the existence across trading countries of differentiated tastes, internal and external economies, product differentiation and intra-industry trade, monopoly power, capital mobility, and technological change and diffusion. What they share in common is the questioning of the dominant role of factor abundance to explain trade, and a greater interest in empirically understanding the reality of multidimensional trade. Indeed, since Leontief's famous study, the nature of world trade has changed dramatically. Historically, most international trade has taken place between more developed countries and less developed countries, and, even in 1953, 62 per cent of the value of exports of more developed countries went to less developed countries. However, by 1990 this figure fell to only 24 per cent (Krugman, 1994: 231). Most international trade today is conducted among more developed countries – the USA, Japan, Europe – and much of trade in manufactures is in intra-industry rather than inter-industry trade. New trade theory is representative of more recent approaches which take these developments into account. In new trade theory, a modified H–O theory provides the necessary but not sufficient conditions for international trade to take place between countries (Krugman, 1994: 233–4). Each country has a number of resources the relative abundance of which shapes the possibilities for trade with other countries. However, this does not imply the export of any particular goods. That depends on the historical circumstances that shaped the development of industries (i.e.

path dependence), the possibilities of increasing returns to scale in expanding an industry, and the existence of in-country external economies of scale to lower resource costs (Krugman, 1994: 226–44). In contrast H–O theory assumes no path dependence, constant returns to scale in all industries and no external economies of scale.

The attempted resolution of the Leontief paradox provides an excellent example of the way mainstream economists deal with unexpected empirical findings, generating additional ideas, theories and empirical work while not rejecting an attractive theory. Leontief's paradox has led economists away from a singular reliance on the factor abundance of H–O theory, loosening its assumptions, and creating more complex theories that describe more fully the reality we observe. At the same time economists have been unwilling to give up on H–O theory completely because, unlike Ricardian comparative advantage, it is embedded in general equilibrium theory, the core of mainstream economics. This has led trade theory into a much deeper empirical direction, prompting studies to gather new data and reconceive both old and new data in an attempt to resolve the Leontief paradox. Not only is this ironic, it may be dialectic. As earlier noted, mainstream economics is theory-driven, not empirically driven, and it was the theoretical inconsistency of H–O theory with general equilibrium theory in the light of Leontief's results that prompted the greater empirical intensity of research to eliminate this inconsistency. That has not happened to date but it is clear, with hindsight, that it has been a research agenda that would not otherwise have been pursued. Indeed, the unfinished story of the Leontief paradox provides, at the very least, strong evidence of the path dependence of academic research.

K.C.T.

REFERENCES

Appleyard, Dennis R. and Alfred J. Field, Jr (1995), *International Economics*, 2nd edn, Chicago, Illinois: Irwin.

DeMarchi, Neil (1976), 'Anomaly and the Development of Economics: the Case of the Leontief Paradox', in Spiro J. Latsis (ed.), *Method and Appraisal in Economics*, Cambridge, UK: Cambridge University Press.

Ethier, Wilfred (1995), *Modern International Economics*, 3rd edn, New York: W.W. Norton.

Heckscher, Eli (1949), 'The Effect of Foreign Trade on the Distribution of Income', reprinted in American Economic Association, *Readings in the Theory of International Trade*, Philadelphia, Pennsylvania: Blakiston, ch. 13. Originally in Swedish in *Ekonomisk Tidskrift*, **21** (1919), 497–512.

Krugman, Paul (1994), *Peddling Prosperity*, New York: W.W. Norton.
Leontief, Wassily (1956), 'Factor Proportions and the Structure of American Trade: Further Theoretical and Empirical Analysis', *Review of Economics and Statistics*, **38** (4), 392–7.
Ohlin, Bertil (1933), *Interregional and International Trade*, Cambridge, Massachusetts: Harvard University Press.

44. The perversity of Wall Street

*'Strong employment gains tend to be negative for both stocks and bonds',
states Marty Zweig, a Wall Street wizard* (The Zweig Forecast, *29 July
1994*). *'A robust economy could hurt stocks', reports* The Wall Street
Journal. *'That's because a robust economy probably would drive up
short-term interest rates, causing investors to dump stocks in favor of the
improving yields on safer, fixed-income investments'* (Wall Street Journal,
13 December 1993, C1). *Yet stock prices are ultimately determined by
earnings and profits, which in turn suggest a robust economy. How do
you explain this perversity of Wall Street?*

GDP rises 5 per cent? The market dives. Unemployment jumps to 7
per cent? Bonds rally. Why is good news on Main Street bad news on
Wall Street? And vice versa? Financial analysts and institutional investors are convinced that 'too strong' economic performance is bad for
the financial markets, and signs of weakness are good.

At the same time, however, it has long been held by financial economists that stock prices are determined by earnings performance over
the long term. As David Dreman declares, 'Research has demonstrated
that earnings and dividends are the most important determinants of
stock prices over time' (Dreman, 1982: 40). And companies can't maintain high earnings and dividends if the economy is in recession. Hence
the puzzle.

According to a *New York Times* article ('Why America Won't Boom',
12 June 1994), the real culprits are the bondholders. 'The American
economy is governed by the bond market', Louis Uchitelle writes, and
'the confederation [of bondholders] has ruled in recent months that the
economy should lose strength, not gain it.' Another recession may not
be good for the country, but it's great for bondholders as interest rates
decline and bond prices rise.

But the puzzle is much more complex than that. For example, there
have been many times in the past when strong economic performance
propelled higher stock prices. The 1920s, the 1950s, early 1960s, and the
1980s are classic examples. In 1960–65, for example, the United States
had a robust economic growth rate of nearly 5 per cent annually, while
the Dow Jones Industrial Average climbed 41 per cent (Brown, 1991:

83–7). During this time period long-term interest rates were relatively stable. Yields on corporate bonds stayed around 4.5 per cent (Homer, 1977: 360).

In the 1980s, stocks rallied sharply in the face of higher economic growth rates, coupled with lower interest rates and inflation (Brown, 1991: 100–112).

Some emerging markets in Latin America and Europe have recently enjoyed higher economic growth in the face of lower interest rates and lower inflation, and stock prices have in turned headed upward.

In short, high economic growth can be sustained without inflation and higher interest rates, and when that happens, the stock market responds favourably.

However, over the past few years, investment analysts have become suspicious of high economic growth or good job reports. Why? Because they fear that it reflects an inflationary boom, an artificial recovery created primarily by 'easy credit'. Strong economic performance data can only mean higher inflation down the road, they assume, which in turn will force the Federal Reserve to tighten money and raise interest rates. Thus stocks and bonds decline on economic news that is 'too good'.

Is future inflation a legitimate fear on Wall Street? Charles R. Nelson, economics professor at the University of Washington, has studied the impact of price inflation, as measured by the consumer price index, and formulated the following trading rule: 'When inflation [as measured by the CPI] is on the rise, stay out of stocks; when it is on the decline, buy stocks' (Nelson, 1987: 123). Nelson showed that the stock market suffered when the CPI trended upward and recovered when the CPI trended steady or downward.

To a large extent the issue hinges on the relevance of monetary policy, whether the Federal Reserve engages in 'easy money' or 'tight money'. If a strong economic recovery is spurred primarily by an easy-money/low-interest rate strategy by the Federal Reserve, the fear of inflation is very real when the economy heats up. Hence interest rates tend to rise once an inflationary boom gets started. Signs of higher inflation tend to make the market nervous.

In short, the only time good economic news is bad news on Wall Street is when the good news is perceived as tainted. If the growth rate or job creation is viewed as temporary due to artificial 'easy-money' policies, market analysts should be sceptical of the good news. It cannot last. But if the economic growth is legitimate and sustainable, investors who overreact and dump stocks are making a serious error.

M.S.

REFERENCES

Brown, John Dennis (1991), *101 Years on Wall Street: An Investor's Almanac*, Englewood Cliffs, New Jersey: Prentice-Hall.

Dreman, David (1982), *The New Contrarian Investment Strategy*, New York: Random House.

Homer, Sidney (1977), *A History of Interest Rates*, 2nd edn, New Brunswick, New Jersey: Rutgers University Press.

Nelson, Charles R. (1987), *The Investor's Guide to Economic Indicators*, New York: John Wiley.

Index